WHAT DO I SAY NEXT?

ALSO BY SUSAN ROANE

How to Work a Room

The Secrets of Savvy Networking

WHAT DO I SAY NEXT?

TALKING YOUR WAY TO BUSINESS AND SOCIAL SUCCESS

SUSAN RoANE

WARNER BOOKS

A Time Warner Company

Warner Books, Inc., 1271 Avenue of the Americas, New York, NY 10020

 A Time Warner Company

Printed in the United States of America
First Printing: August 1997
10 9 8 7 6 5 4 3 2 1

Library of Congress Cataloging-in-Publication Data

RoAne, Susan
    What do I say next? : talking your way to business and
social success / Susan RoAne.
      p. cm.
    Includes bibliographical references and index.
    ISBN 0-446-52000-4
    1. Conversation. I. Title.
BJ2121.R63   1997
302.3'46—DC20   96-43903
                                   CIP

Book design and composition by L&G McRee

TO MY FRIENDS

. . . whose words have woven the fabric of our friendship

TO DR. GERALDINE ALPERT

. . . whose wisdom, words, and laughter gave rise to the evolution of this Susan

ACKNOWLEDGMENTS

Writing a book on talking meant I was so busy writing that I often couldn't have extensive conversations with people. Nevertheless, no book is a solitary effort and I am deeply grateful to those who helped with this one.

Thanks to my audiences, clients, colleagues, and network for their assistance, support, insights, and ideas—and for the time they took for surveys, interviews, and laughter. Thanks, too, to those of you who said, "Of course, you're the perfect person to write a book on conversation!"

My heartfelt gratitude and love to my friends. Each of you brainstormed and birthed the book with me:

- Becky Gordon for translating the handwritten hieroglyphics without a Rosetta stone and for those discussions about transitive verbs and the like . . . for editing and editing, and for the Gordon Giggle Test.
- Lana Teplick for longtime best friendship and the "Oh Wow! That's great!" every time I finished another chapter. And especially for first-draft feedback.
- Joyce (Mumsy) Siegel for time, encouragement, laughter, and love.

Acknowledgments

- Carl LaMell (the Boss) for business advice, friendship, and for bringing the voice of reason into my dual-career world—and for giving direction to this book.
- Patricia Fripp for being a mentor, role model, speaker extraordinaire, and friend.
- Lois Vieira, longtime friend, whose perspective has contributed to my growth and who has taught me a few signs . . . to help me communicate.
- Sherwood Cummins, personal trainer and minister, for talking me through the book while ministering to my muscles.
- Michael LeBoeuf, for being a friend and matchmaker with Artie Pine.
- Carol Costello, sculptor, editor, friend, and fellow fighting Illini.

Merci, muchas gracias, todah rabah, grazie, danke schön, Thank You. Thanks, too, to all of you who have allowed me to quote and share you and your stories with audiences and readers. (And once again, thanks to the irksome conversationalists who provided tips on what *not* to say or do.)

Thanks to the crews at Spinelli's Coffee Company for double decaf espresso "Depth Charges" that charged me up to write from the "depth of my soul."

To Gabriella Castenetto for being the "messenger service" and rescue squad.

To Syl, David, Dan, P.J., John, Diane, Shelly, Michael, Lisa, Marcie, Gert, Shirley, Patrick, and Beej. You each know your contribution to the conversation of my life. And to Lil and the late Nate, my parents, may you continue to *kvell* (see Glossary) in your conversations wherever you may be.

And to the Skovs—Terri, Pete, Patrick, and Shayne— for support, love, hugs, and for grounding "Grandma

Susan." Especially to Terri, who said, "Get your pencil, go into the dining room, and start writing a chapter about this event." I did.

And to my favorite nanny, Fran Drescher, for my weekly dose of hilarity (and Yiddish).

Thanks to my editor formerly at Warner Books, Joann Davis, who believed the world needed and was ready for my book on conversation. And to my agent, Artie Pine, so respected and admired in the world of publishing.

And to you, the book buyers, the readers . . . the people who really made this book possible. Nice chatting with you, and thanks!

CONTENTS

Contents

Contents

Contents

AN OPEN LETTER TO MISS KELLY

Dear Miss Kelly,

I really liked your first grade a lot. You were a very good and nice teacher. Except you gave me lots of red checks on my report card because I didn't keep "profitably busy." I was restless, but my work was always done before I left my seat to talk to my classmates.

Then you told my mother that I should skip second grade, but that you wouldn't double-promote me because I talked too much to my friends during class.

Miss Kelly, I still talk a lot—and really profitably. I still talk to Barry P., Shelly E., Esther F., and Judy L.—and now I get to share in this book some of those "red check" strategies that have served me so well.

I am glad you were nice and did not kill my spirit.

Sincerely,
Susan RoAne
(4th row, 2nd seat)
PS: I liked second grade anyway.

INTRODUCTION

The art of conversation is not going to die. It may change, expand, or move to new locations—but it is not going to die. We are now talking in the bleachers, in coffeehouses, in book clubs, and on-line. *Conversation is the core of communication, the key component in leadership and overall success.*

Verbal fluency is linked to success in many ways: giving speeches, on the phone, face-to-face, video conferencing, participation in meetings, and conversations in both business and in social/business situations. These conversations are the focus of this book.

The Verbal Edge provides the keys to converse with ease in many circumstances: board retreats, client meetings, trade shows, fund-raisers and the myriad social occasions we attend in our personal lives. It also offers the phrases, thoughts and scripts for those difficult situations in life where we are called upon to give words of comfort, empathy and support. And it includes a compendium of "ice-melters," which bridge communication gaps and build rapport and relationships.

Think of the most congenial, easygoing conversation-

1

alist you know. What is it that makes him or her so easy to talk to? How do you feel, respond, and act around these ConverSensations™? What do they do? What do they say? Would you like to converse as confidently as they do and be as comfortable as they are in conversation?

The good news is that we already have the tools to do this—**WORDS!** The even better news is that successful, confident conversation is possible for all of us. It is within our reach as long as we prepare, practice, pay attention to and respect others, and make a personal commitment to developing our conversational prowess.

Even shyness doesn't have to hold us back. Eighty-eight percent of us self-identify as shy in one form or another, according to Dr. Philip Zimbardo, author of *Shyness: What It Is, What to Do About It.* Being shy just means that we are reluctant or uncomfortable in conversation—*not* that we are incompetent. This book provides insights, ideas, tips, and techniques that can make anyone a ConverSensation.

In preparing this book, I conducted an extensive survey on conversation among CEOs, senior executives, ConverSensations, and great communicators from all walks of life, age groups, professions, and geographical areas to find out what works for them. These people "cover the waterfront." They are software geniuses, insurance magnates, scientists, clergy, academics, Ph.D.s, M.D.s, L.L.B.s, C.P.A.s, and O.G.P.s (Other Great People).

There are no hard and fast rules about conversation— at least none that really work. We can't do quantitative scientific double-blind studies to produce conversation formulas that work every time, because every conversation is fluid and unique to those people, that time, and that place. Conversation is a function of who is involved, what is happening for each person at that particular moment in time, the chemistry between them, and the lifetime experiences of everybody in the conversation.

Good conversation is an ART. It has a flow, a fluidity that defies scientific analysis. It is organic. A great conversation cannot adhere to a specific outline or formula. When we know exactly what we want to say, it's called a speech.

While words are very important, *how* we say those words—tone, pause, inflection, body language, gestures, facial expression, pacing—gives them context and makes for comfortable, confident conversation that leaves us feeling good. Much of our conversation, verbal and otherwise, comes out of our sensitivity to other people, and our ability to follow our own good instincts in the moment.

Those of us who study conversation can offer guidelines and food for thought, but **each of us has to learn to listen and respond to what is said**—and what is *not* said. What works in one situation may not work in another. But we can learn some basic strategies, and some basic attitudes about how we *treat people* that make for effective and happy conversations.

The Verbal Edge is about becoming more successful in all areas of life by mastering the delicate but powerful art of conversation, It is rooted in common sense—and is practical, irreverent, and sometimes opinionated.

Whether you are a CEO, contractor, doctor, carpenter, engineer, producer, salesperson, Little League coordinator, local arts council member . . . whether you are beginning, managing, or changing careers . . . whether you are a fund-raising chairperson or a hair-raising fun person . . . whether you are an introverted shy person or an outgoing extrovert . . . I wrote this book for you.

After reading it, you'll always be able to answer Joan Rivers' rhetorical "Can we talk?" with a resounding "Yes!"

We've even provided a Yiddish Glossary at the end of the book to define terms in the *Yinglish* of today's world.

Conversation takes practice; the more we do it, the better we get, and the more easily we do it. Confidence and comfort build, and so does our personal and professional success.

The Verbal Edge offers a smorgasbord of ideas. Try some that feel comfortable, then try some others that don't. Change works best when we want to make it. The purpose of this book is to make you feel more comfortable and confident and, ultimately, more successful!

CHAPTER 1

SCHMOOZE OR LOSE: WHY WE NEED CONVERSATION TO SUCCEED

"To what skill do you most attribute your success?"

I asked this question of all the successful people I interviewed for this book. Their number one answer was: THE ABILITY TO CONVERSE!

If you want to be successful, we don't get to choose whether or not to develop and enhance our conversation prowess. *SCHMOOZE OR LOSE* is the rule for both personal and professional success.

Formal research from Harvard to Stanford and places in between supports my informal findings that the ability to converse and communicate is a key factor in success. A survey of managers sponsored by the National Association of Colleges and Employees rated "oral communication skills" as the most important.

As corporations continue to merge and jobs disappear, we need conversation and communication more than ever before. Networks of loyal customers and relationships become pivotal. We establish, develop, and nurture those relations by our actions, but also by our exchanges and our *conversation.*

PAY ATTENTION is the watchword for the millennium.

Pay attention to projects, to details, to trends, and most of all *to people.*

UNEQUIVOCAL EQUATION

In the early 1990s, Dr. Thomas Harrell, Professor Emeritus of Business at Stanford University, studied a group of M.B.A.s a decade after their graduation. His goal was to identify the traits of those who were most successful.

He found that grade point average had no bearing on success. The one trait he identified in common among the "successfuls" was their *verbal fluency.* They were confident conversationalists who could talk to anyone: colleagues, investors, strangers, bosses, or associates. They could speak well in front of audiences, and they were easy to talk to.

The unequivocal equation:
VERBAL FLUENCY = SUCCESS AND AFFLUENCY.

CONFIDENT CONVERSATION

Conversation is the basis of communication. It establishes rapport and connects us to our colleagues, clients, cronies, competitors, co-workers, subordinates, superiors, and friends.

Our conversation skills are vital, and they will become even more so in the future. In the late 1980s, Dr. Nathan Keyfitz, Professor Emeritus of Sociology at Harvard, concluded that in the year 2000 most people will be technically adept, *but those who succeed will be the "people who can talk to people."*

The confident conversationalists will set themselves apart even more than they do today. Knowing what to say

6

first, and what to say next, moves us to the next step of our careers.

THE QUINTESSENTIAL QUIZ

In this quiz, there is only one question: **Do you like people?**

If your answer is yes, you are already ahead of the game. Liking people is the heart of good conversation. If you find people nice, helpful, interesting, or informative—you will *want* to talk with them. They will know that, and like it. You've already connected with them, and scored points.

If you answered no, read on anyway! Once you learn to converse more comfortably and start getting positive responses, you may change your mind. When you feel more confident in conversation, relating to people becomes much easier and more pleasant. That attitude leads to success in both business and personal relationships.

Confidence in your ability to converse makes you a better manager, supervisor, employer and colleague. It's worth a try! In *Oh, God! You Devil,* George Burns' co-star discovers he is God and asks, "Should I pray to you?" Burns gives him the same advice I would give you: "It couldn't hurt!"

THE SOUL OF THE WIT ... LESS

When Shakespeare wrote "Brevity is the soul of wit," he did not mean to provide a rationalization for clamming up and not extending ourselves to others under the pretense of being a person "of few words."

None of us wants to be confused with those who play the tough, hard-to-get "game" of monosyllabic responses. Whatever these people are asked, they respond in cryptic monosyllables—"Yup," "No," "Uh," or "Nuh"—and actually seem to enjoy watching people squirm. We rarely hear anyone speak glowingly of these folks.

Some people sneer at "small talk" and dismiss it as banal or trivial. They take pride in being urgent, bottom-line, get-to-the-point, terse people—people who have "more important things on their mind" than small talk. Some of us are naturally terser than others, but none of us can afford not to be conversationalists.

When we can't be bothered to be pleasant, we convey an inflated sense of our own importance—when, in fact, our urgency and gruffness may just mask a lack of confidence. Life and work flow more smoothly when we are comfortable with conversation and know how to make others feel comfortable as well.

DON'T SAVE NANOSECONDS

Other people can't be bothered with small talk because it's "a waste of time." Saving nanoseconds by eliminating connections with people makes no sense at all—in business or in our personal lives.

By the time we leave the planet, we may have saved an hour. Big deal. If we invest in those moments in the pleasantries or small talk that establishes rapport, we'll probably be both happier and richer.

"People do business with people they know, like, and trust," according to John Naisbitt and Patricia Aburdene in *Reinventing the Corporation.* Conversation, even casual conversation, makes sense. It helps us know our clients, potential clients, colleagues, co-workers, and friends.

When we say we don't want to waste time with small talk, we suggest that we don't want to invest time getting a sense of the other person—his interests, her takes on things, or his communication patterns and preferences. It hints that we're too busy, or too disinterested, to bother with that person.

SMALL TALK IS BIG

Small talk is the way to connect even in situations where "big talk"—murder, war, famine, pestilence, and Papal Edict No. 123—may not always be appropriate. Not everyone wants to hear our views on the deadly ebola virus or the latest border skirmish at a museum fundraiser for students of the arts. The big issues are important, but we must know the right time or place for them.

Small talk is the biggest talk we do. It builds, develops, and nurtures relationships. Conversation is how we strengthen the safety net of people who make up our personal and professional networks, our Rolodex™ of sources and resources.

Small talk is how we exchange information, preferences, ideas, and opinions on issues. It's how we break the ice and get a sense of what people are, what they like, and what they *are* like. And it doesn't always have to be about "small" subjects. I've often seen people getting to know one another by having casual conversations about art, sports, economics, government programs, or health issues.

Small talk is what we do to build the big talk. It is the schmoozing that cements relationships and success.

THE DEADLY TALKERS SOCIETY

Conversation requires political savvy. Nancy Shina, president of Millennium Marketing, has found that to be true in her two-decade career in the hospitality industry, where she rose from sales assistant to corporate vice president.

"Conversation is politics. One must be aware of what can or cannot be discussed, should or should not be discussed, and with whom that conversation should or shouldn't occur. When we think things through and have schmooze topics prepared, we are less likely to say the wrong thing to the wrong person."

> *"Good conversation is to die for; lousy conversation is to die from."*
> —UNKNOWN

THE FISHING TRIP ... REMEMBER TO BAIT THE HOOK

The Five Ps can keep you out of the Deadly Talkers Society. Just remember the old army saw: *Prior Planning Prevents Poor Performance.* It's a military axiom that applies nicely to our conversation skills.

Conversation is a natural, enjoyable human activity, but it works even better with just a little attention and planning. Bill Newton, CEO of Norcal Insurance, was invited on a three-day fishing trip in Western Canada with five other CEOs. "I had not known any of the other CEOs before, but I had read a lot about one of the men whom I wanted to meet who had successfully done something I want our company to do. For the first few days I fished, chatted, and listened. On the third day, I went out on the boat with the guy I wanted to get to know. The day was great and we've made plans to continue our dialogue." That conversation started with boats and bait, but led to business.

Bill Newton was *prepared,* had an *agenda* (part of which was catching fish), and did his *homework.* Fishing was something he had in common with the man he wanted to meet. Their host was another. The conversations moved easily to other "fishing holes" (trips), other sports, special interests—and subtly, when appropriate, to business.

Let's face it. Improving our ability to converse with other human beings helps us get more out of life—more business, more friends, more significant relationships of all kinds. It's a lesson I learned as a child, when I went with my dad to paper industry conventions in Miami where I learned to "work" the pool rather than swim in it!

Life is an exchange of energy, and conversation is one of the primary ways we play catch with one another. Those who know how to converse with ease and skill play the game better and have more fun.

REMINDERS

- Conversation is an art, not a science.
- If you like people, you've won half the battle for more conversational prowess.
- The ability to schmooze contributes to personal and professional success.
- Small talk is the most important talk we can do.

CHAPTER 2

THE BANQUET OF BANTER
IS A POTLUCK

The banquet of banter is a potluck—but not a self-serving one. This means we all must contribute some substantial, well-prepared, satisfying morsels. Some of us may supply the meat and potatoes, others the vegetables. Still others bring the appetizers, the (just) desserts, or the whine.

The potluck is interesting, varied, and substantial because everyone contributes something different. If we partake, we'll be satisfied. But if we hang back in the corner, or don't eat because we didn't bring anything, we may walk away hungry for the company, information, ideas, and laughter that are part of good conversation.

The possibilities of the potluck are plentiful. Our conversation can whet people's appetites, and enhance both our "presence and presents" to the banquet of banter.

This chapter is about planning and preparing our contribution to the conversation potluck. There are infinite varieties of delicious dishes—and we can find them in the most unexpected places.

THE "GENEROUS" COP-OUT

I often hear people say that their conversational secret is to ask lots of questions and let the other people talk about themselves. After all, "It's everyone's favorite subject." This view is especially common among salespeople who have attended the "investigative style of conversation as needs assessment" seminars. It drives me wild because:

- It doesn't work.
- It is manipulative.
- It doesn't ring true. (This approach frequently comes across as, "I'm not interested in you; just the stats I need to perfect my sales pitch.")
- It can make people feel as if they're being investigated, not conversed with—and that isn't palatable.

Chandler Tagliabue is a vice president of "Christmas in April * USA," a nonprofit that provides volunteer home renovation services for low-income home owners. She attends functions across the country with her spouse, Paul, the commissioner of the National Football League.

"I get so tired of being asked the same questions over and over by people who think that I am my favorite subject," she says. "There are many topics I find interesting. Frankly, I already know my own story! It's always a pleasure when I get the chance to speak with people who also have something to share and will converse on a wide range of issues."

CPA Lorraine Ferrarese was also frustrated by a new acquaintance who was acting like an inquisitor. "She is always 'in your face,' asking a lot of questions. While some people think it shows interest, I don't! She *never listens to an answer* before going on to her next question."

Editorial Director Mark Chimsky of Harper San

Francisco is a terrific conversationalist. Once he asks a question, he listens to the answer. "I think it's important to listen, to pick up on the small cues that are usually there and to use them to actively engage someone in a dialogue. I love to make the surprising connection, finding out what I share in common with someone else—and if we don't agree on something, to find out why," he says.

Mark is a genius at building a verbal exchange, but what about the rest of us? How do we know what to bring to the potluck? Where can we get the ingredients? And where did we put that recipe box?

PLANNING FOR THE POTLUCK

When we're invited to a potluck, we think about what dish we'll bring *before* we get in the car to drive to the event. If we didn't, everyone would drop by the market at the last minute and the table would be a sea of chips and dips. That's not what we want for our conversation.

Planning ahead allows us to bring better dishes to the table, and to feel more confident about them. Here are four things you can do to prepare your dish:

POTLUCK PREPARATION

1. Plan three items, issues or stories to share.
2. Plan four generic questions to ask.
3. Use the newspaper, experiences (yours and others'), current events, books, tournaments and movies as subjects.
4. Think about each item or issue—its ramifications, questions it raises, your opinions about it.

When all else fails, here is a question that always gets people's attention and creates great conversation:
If you could be doing something else, what would that be? Why?
The response to this question not only gives you wonderful insight into people, but can become the focus of the evening.

THE BASIC INGREDIENTS: WHAT INTERESTS YOU?

What we do, know, observe, think, and question . . . what we find unique, amazing, and informative are the tempting conversational morsels that call to us most strongly.

We all have different tastes and interests, just as we have different preferences in food. Some of these tastes are instinctive, and others are acquired through exposure and willingness to experiment. I found unagi (eel), my favorite type of sushi, this way.

We're likely to be most enthusiastic and best informed about our own "hummers" or favorites. This may make us most fascinating when we talk about these things—but it can backfire if we're not sensitive to others' tastes and preferences. Not everybody cares for eel. I can offer it, but I make sure I have some alternatives as backup.

A SAMPLE PLATTER

At many family restaurants, they have a dish known as the "Fisherman's Platter" that contains little bits of all the seafood served at the restaurant. It's for those who like variety, can't make up their minds, or just want to sample everything that's available.

Conversation is a great way to "try on other people's lives," find out what the world is offering them this week, and sample a little taste of everything. More than 75 percent of the savvy socializers I've surveyed over the years said that they look forward to both business and social events because the people they meet there have so much to offer. **They see talking to people as a way to learn new things.**

Remember that you are one of the people they look forward to meeting, and that what makes a potluck dish successful is quality, not quantity. Think about what satisfying morsels, tidbits, and food for thought and conversation you want to bring to the party, and be generous. Also, don't forget to enjoy what other people bring, and perhaps even take some home with you.

"Words should be weighed, not counted."
—AN OBSERVER OF ELECTIONS IN ISRAEL

INCIDENTAL CONVERSATION

All conversation is about life, and life happens *to* us and *around* us—all day, every day. There is no shortage of material. The stories and vignettes of fascinating conversation are everywhere we look.

We even have unlimited RAM (random access memory) with which to remember these funny or poignant incidents. Without unlimited RAM, how would we frame those obscure *Jeopardy!* questions? Or remember the smell of Grandmother's egg bread, or gnocchi, or wonton soup wafting through the house?

We may have occasional glitches and outages, but we have more than the eight bytes of RAM needed to run Windows '95—even if we "don't do windows."

MEMORIES ARE MADE OF THIS: A FOUR-PART PROCESS

How can we better remember the interesting events, moments, and stories? Try this four-part system:

1. **Focus** on what you just saw and heard. Review it in your mind.
2. **Write it down!** Humorist Jeanne Robertson keeps "Jeanne's Journal." These are not jokes or "borrowed" stories. They are her observations and incidents collected from cab drivers, bell staff, clients, etc. She writes them down so she *knows* she won't forget them!
3. **Read your notes.**
4. **Practice telling these stories** to friends, relatives, and the mirror.

SPIRALING STORIES

Keep a small spiral-bound notebook. It costs less than a dollar and fits easily into a pocket or purse. It doesn't require batteries, chips, modems, or booting up.

When something happens that's interesting or noteworthy, jot down the date, the people involved, and key words to capture the essence of the event. Like a good reporter, get the "where, when, who, what and why."

Then write down the punch line or irony that caught your attention. What was clever, poignant, or funny? Who said what? What was the import or impact of that comment? Ask permission to use it, and give credit to the source. Who could say no to your "That was brilliant! May I write it and credit you?"

A "SOURCE" SPOT

Good conversationalists reference their material and give credit where credit is due. It's no skin off their noses to say:

- "I read the most interesting perspective in a *Wired* article by Jonathan Katz. He believes that . . ."
- "Judge Michael Goodman had the strangest experience at a conference in Salt Lake City . . ."
- "My five-year-old said the funniest thing when he was using the computer . . ."
- "Diane Bennett made a poignant observation about the baby boomers . . ."
- "Oh, you're a quilter? How did you develop the skill? My friend Becky Gordon just won first prize in the Marin Quilt Show."

Crediting your sources is classy, appropriate, and demonstrates integrity. The light always spills over onto us when we shine it on others.

THE PROCESS OF POTLUCK

Like a potluck meal, conversation is a process that progresses. We move from course to course, or discourse to discourse.

The move from appetizer to salad is signaled by the completion of the appetizer: fork on the (clean) plate, prongs down. In conversation, we don't always have clear visual signals when it's time to move on to the next "discourse." We have to keep our eyes and ears open, and our antennae up—reading body language, observing facial expression, and having a sense of when a particular subject or conversation is over.

How do we move on or to the next topic or conversation? The "Sultans of Segue" move with a subtle flow that continues the seamless process of the banquet—often using the phrases and tips below.

SUPPLYING THE MISSING LINKS

These magic phrases, responses, and general comments create bridges and start building the next conversation. Some of them are also handy for sidestepping or diffusing difficult people.

- "I hadn't thought of it that way. How did you come to that?"
- "That's a new way of looking at it."
- "It reminds me of . . ."
- "It depends on perspective. _____ (a famous person or someone you know in common) might say . . ."
- "How interesting! I'd like to learn about that."
- And the ubiquitous "Tell me more."

CHOCOLATE CHIPS ... OFF THE OLD BLOCK

Conversation is like a chocolate chip cookie—rich, melt-in-your-mouth doughy presence studded with stunning chunks of exciting words.

Although a lot of people use the Toll House chocolate chip recipe, some people make better Toll House cookies than others. One difference is the number of chocolate chips they use. Some have just the right amount, some don't have enough, and—although this may be hard to believe—some have too many! There are so many chips, there's hardly any cookie around them. Sometimes we talk so much, use so many words, that our conversation partners feel overwhelmed. We don't want to be stingy bakers. Better to be generous, but avoid overkill.

In *The Givers and the Takers,* Cris Evatt and Bruce Feld specify talkers as Givers of words. These Givers are generous in sharing their conversation, their energy, and themselves—but the verbose give too much, choking us on chocolate chips so that we must run away to *get milk.* The Takers, on the other hand, are stingy. They give less of themselves and their chocolate chip words.

GIVERS AND TAKERS

Givers—give words.
Takers—accept them and only give back when it will help them help themselves.

21

DON'T FORGET NUTRITION

Although vitamins and minerals, proteins and carbohydrates may be the last thing on our minds when we head off for a potluck, a steady diet of brownies and puff pastry eventually leaves us a little weak.

Action is the nutrition behind our words. Like Eliza Doolittle in *My Fair Lady,* we may want to sing "Words, words, words, I'm so sick of words" if they are *not* supported by deeds. Words are important. They can inspire, anger, embarrass, or praise. But **behavior that does not support words, subverts them.**

If someone's positive, upbeat, energetic words ring falsely on a gut level, they probably are! Whether that person is a client, co-worker, sibling, or chum, be just as cautious as you would around food that gives you indigestion or causes an allergic reaction. I recently let a "fan" become a friend because her words were great to hear. But her words were empty and there was no follow-through. **Trust your gut** to eliminate the stomachache—and heartache.

By the same token, we should be sure our words are "golden"—filled with the nutrition of good intention, and backed up by our behavior.

"DISHING UP" SPICES

Warning: "Dishing" and "dissing" others fall into the category of "hot, spicy foods." They can backfire and cause indigestion, so use them gingerly.

For some people, no subject is off limits. For others, many are. The banquet of banter can be enhanced by hot spices, but we should be careful and blend them "to taste."

Variety, as in "variety is the spice of life," is a safer brand of spice. Interesting conversation includes questions, expressions of enthusiasm, information, and listening. Each variety of contribution has its own tone.

The magic is in the mix, which keeps us from being typecast as a certain type of talker.

THE DEPARTMENT OF CORRECTIONS

Sometimes we inhibit our conversation by wanting everything we say to be correct, articulate, and brilliant. We want to sound profound. We want to use perfect grammar. We want to say it in the best possible way. While we wait to say the perfect thing, we say nothing. And we miss opportunities.

Good conversation is an interesting exchange that can be thoughtful and thought-provoking, fun, informative, and even inspire us to action. But it is never *perfect*. There is no such thing as perfection in conversation, because there is no linear measurement for it. Conversation is a work of art that is always "in progress."

Courteous conversation partners do not correct others—certainly not in public, and perhaps not even in private.

We're all doing the best we can, and none of us is perfect. If you feel uncomfortable because you're not sure about certain words or usages, find out the answers so that you can share your insights, your questions, and your zest for life in conversation.

THE BUSINESS MEAL BANQUET

Conversation at business meals should have a focus, and yet be fluid enough to include small talk as appropriate.

When we agree to a meeting that happens over a meal, we give our tacit approval to social conversation prior to the "meat of the matter." Otherwise, we should schedule the meeting in an office, over the phone, or by fax or modem. Remember, there is always time to converse, build rapport, and develop your relationship with the other person. Increasingly, this is the stuff of which business is made.

As always, preparation and planning are key. Use this six-point plan to manage the meal deal:

ROANE'S SIX-POINT PLAN FOR THE MEAL DEAL

1. Be prepared.
2. Know the company.
3. Read their corporate literature and financial report.
4. Prepare conversation: a mixture of observations, questions, revelations, vignettes from the newspaper, and industry chatter.
5. Listen, listen, listen.
6. Respond accordingly. Remember etiquette and the manners of doing business and meals.

MOVING FROM EATING TO MEETING

When do you make the leap from pleasantries and small talk to the business, or "meat," of the meal?

It depends entirely on your guest or client. Most often the move to business is after the main course is cleared. But with a busy person who has allotted only seventy-five to ninety minutes for the entire event, you may need to move your agenda forward. Again, it's important to read people, pay attention to their verbal and nonverbal communications—and follow the cues they give.

MANGEZ A TROIS

If there are several people at the lunch or dinner, we need to include them all through eye contact and speaking directly to each individual. Focusing our gaze only on the person(s) across the table exclude the people sitting next to us—not a behavior that "serves" us.

If spouses are present, respect and include them with eye contact and conversation.

ACT LIKE A HOST

The right attitude will get you through any difficulty and answer any question that comes up. In conversation and mingling, you can't go wrong when you act like a host.

The host's first job is to make guests feel comfortable. We can build this rapport through conversation and showing interest in our companions. Where are they from? Where did they go to school? What are their outside interests? Do they have children? What brought them to the area?

We can offer the same kind of information about ourselves. People do business with people they know, like, and trust—and conversation is the core of the "getting to know you."

As a host, you may also be in charge of making the arrangements for the gathering. If you choose the restaurant, select a place that is conducive to conversation and business.

Jonathan is an advertising executive who told me he joined San Francisco's City Club for just that purpose. "I had been taking clients to a well-known financial district restaurant, but I was always treated with something less than enthusiasm there," he says. "The greetings were flat, and there was never a word of appreciation for my patronage. Even though I ate there two or three times a month, they never seemed to recognize me. Who needs it? At the City Club, my guests and I are greeted warmly, and the atmosphere is conducive to business. The food and service are very good, everything is handled discreetly, and there is no bill unceremoniously left on the table."

Hosts don't think of these meetings as competitions. Mike, a partner in a Big Six accounting firm, didn't follow this advice. He said he never took much time with pleasantries and used football terms to describe these business meals. "Winning" the contract, "beating" the competition, and "scoring" points were his themes. Those words all imply a loser, and gracious hosts don't think in terms of vanquishing opponents. Mike's behavior may have met his own needs, but it didn't always match the styles of his clients. The best hosts take their cues from their guests.

DON'T LET THE MEAL GO UP IN SMOKE

We need to be mindful of a "smokin'" issue. Many cities now have ordinances prohibiting smoking in any restaurant, at any time—but even these establishments can permit smoking in adjoining bars. Sometimes there is still a decision to be made.

As a gracious host, you can ask, "Would you prefer smoking or not?"

If you have a strong preference for nonsmoking, you can ask, "Would it work for you if we sat in the non-smoking section?"

But what if your guest or client is a smoker? Is it okay to tell the truth? I've heard people handle the issue this way: "My eyes are sensitive to smoke. Do you mind if we sit in a nonsmoking section?"

Whether you are a smoker or nonsmoker, how to handle smoking at a business meal is a personal issue. The trick is to find a balance of courtesy and tolerance. The people at the top didn't get there by being ill-mannered clods, whether they are smokers or nonsmokers.

You may learn that your client is a cigar aficionado like yourself, in which case you could arrange to attend an Alfred Dunhill Cigar Soiree. This isn't a gender-biased suggestion; the press has paid a lot of attention to female stogie smokers lately.

The watchwords are: **Be aware, be sensitive, and be prepared.** This applies not just to business meals, but to any banquet of banter. At conversation potlucks in private homes, there are usually some smoking rules or smoking areas. If no one in the room is smoking, don't be the first to light up without asking your host or hostess.

RoANE'S RECIPE FROM THE CONVERSATION COOKBOOK

Driving across the Golden Gate Bridge one morning, I had an epiphany . . . a recipe for conversation! This is what you need:

Susan RoAne

RoANE'S RECIPE

BASIC INGREDIENTS:

Words: we all have these in our cupboards
Attitude: positive only
Sincerity: in large doses
Energy: varying levels to taste

Listening: hold the judgments
Combine: seven words, e.g., *"I am interested in assessing your product."*
Add: a period for punctuation.
Sprinkle: with a positive adjective, e.g., *"Really."*
Simmer: over time
You may substitute a question: e.g., *"How can I get information about your product?"*
Fold in: one question mark
Don't **dredge** up past problems
Or **beat** the product failures to death
Mix in: an observation, e.g., *"This year's line is even better than last year's."*
Sprinkle in: a smile
Fold in: one revelation, e.g., *"I prefer the new line because it's more youth oriented."*
Don't **grate** on people's nerves
Pour on: an interjection, e.g., *"Great for sales!"*
Don't **drizzle** zest of two lemons (it will leave a sour taste)
Don't **crush** people's hopes and dreams or
Blanch: when taken by surprise
Blend, Cover, Simmer and let the ingredients **gel**
Season: to taste

28

REMINDERS

- Everyone has to bring a "morsel of conversation" to the banter banquet.
- Merely asking questions is not a contribution, and it's not particularly palatable.
- Our memory capacities need no upgrading.
- Keep a small spiral notebook for recording incidents, stories, jokes, and ideas.
- Reference sources; give credit where credit is due.
- Prepare three items to share and four generic questions to ask.
- The basic ingredients of conversation are WORDS and sentences. Combine them with verbal and facial expression, variations in tone and inflection and pace.
- Mix words and sentences well and you have the basis of banter, and a Recipe for Success!

CHAPTER 3

CONVERSENSATIONS™:
HOW DO THEY DO IT?

ConverSensations are people who enjoy conversation and are very good at it. These people are fun, easy to be around, always interesting, and successful—in part at least because they know how to talk to people.

To understand the secrets of their success, and to get their best advice and most effective hints, I designed and sent surveys to the best ConverSensations I know: friends, colleagues, clients, relations, acquaintances, associates, and even a former "gentleman caller."

This chapter is about what they do, and how they do it—so that all of us can become ConverSensations!

NO TALK IS SMALL TALK

The most significant comment on my survey was the one my ConverSensations did *not* make. *Not one person denigrated "small talk,"* questioned its value, or impugned it as worthless or unimportant. To the contrary, each ConverSensation wrote that finding and talking about common interests was a way to encourage the flow of conversation. The weather, a traffic jam, the convention's keynote speaker, or the client's office furnishings aren't trivial; they can be ways to start and nurture conversations that make others feel at ease. They are tools to build rapport.

John Marks, CEO of the San Francisco Convention and Visitors Bureau as well as a delightful and funny conversational partner, wrote that those who understand the purpose of small talk are good at it because they "love the art."

What makes someone CEO material or gives them the potential to become a leader or partner? Of the seven traits of leaders identified in *Performance* magazine, the ability to communicate was at the top.

THE BOTTOM LINE OF SUCCESS

The other things that all my ConverSensations had in common was that they credited their success to their ability to converse and communicate. The CEOs, the teachers, the union representative, the priest, the scientist, the preacher and the parishioners, the managing partners, and the partners who manage to bring in clients all linked their success to being able to converse.

And they credited conversational prowess not just for their professional success, but also for their personal success. They said their ability to converse brought them better and richer relationships, more friends, more activity, community status, and more invitations to do the things they like.

This makes sense. In his best-selling *Emotional Intelligence,* Daniel Goleman describes the fundamental characteristics of those who have "smarts" that don't register on SATs or IQ tests. They are "most likable, have social poise and a special ability to put people at ease and are comfortable with themselves. They interact smoothly and manage feelings well. They are also conversant."

Bill Newton, CEO of Norcal Insurance, says that "verbal communication is a key strength to convey the application of a new concept or strategy. And personally most useful in expanding horizons and meeting new people."

ConverSensations like P.J. Livingston, senior vice president of an insurance company, have smiles that light up rooms, an infectious laugh, and a lighthearted demeanor. They are serious about what they do—but not terminally so, and not about who they are. Each conveys a sense of what Linda Mantel, Vice President of Wilson Learning, calls "being comfortable in their own skin." Carolyn Layne, Vice President of TeleTV, notes their self-esteem. They are not afraid to share the failure and the faux pas as well as the accomplishments.

Because listening is not enough for a conversation, ConverSensations respond, reveal, and contribute. Al Walker, a professional speaker and sales trainer, has found that "genuine people want to have *meaningful* two-way conversations. So being a listener isn't enough— we need to be both." Amen.

> *"If you are not fired with enthusiasm, you will be fired with enthusiasm."*
> —COACH VINCE LOMBARDI

A SENSE OF HUMOR

Arlynn Greenbaum, President of Authors Unlimited, a speakers bureau, suggests, "Don't forget humor." She doesn't. Arlynn always has a funny story or ironic situation to share—and like many of the ConverSensations, there is always a smile in her voice!

Some ConverSensations tell jokes, and others do not—but all express their sense of humor in some way. Becky Gordon owns Awards on Stage, a trophy and engraving company in San Francisco, and her laughter is part of the charm that makes everyone comfortable with her. Others, like Leslie Taglio, a manufacturer's representative and entrepreneur, laugh at themselves.

THE LOVE OF TALK, PEOPLE, AND LIFE

CEO Maggie Wilderotter of WINK Communications claims you "need a love of people to be a good conversationalist."

ConverSensations genuinely like people. Father Paul Keenan, host of New York Archdiocese's radio show *As You Think,* says, "I enjoy people and their stories and ideas."

Evangeline Ysmael, a freelance journalist, "treats everyone with respect, kindness, and compassion" regardless of whether or not they represent a business opportunity. It is also natural for good conversationalists to "listen, listen, listen," according to Dan Donovan, Vice President of Dean Witter.

ConverSensations share high animation and convey a sense of energy—both as talkers and as listeners.

Dr. Stanley Schainker, consultant for the Center for Creative Leadership in Greensboro, North Carolina, is a longtime friend. He has been a school superintendent and professor, and most recently, directed a leadership development program at Duke University.

His top tip: Listen carefully to what is said and *not* said, and don't rush into value judgments.

Many ConverSensations started out shy, but all of them mastered and learned to love the art of conversation. Because they are well-informed, they never lack for something to say. Author, speaker, and executive image consultant Diane Parente says they "read a lot, especially daily newspapers. There is always something about which to talk."

Like Rod Beckstrom, CEO of CATS Software, ConverSensations have "plenty of outside interests to touch upon." Many play golf, poker, or tennis. They may listen to Verdi, fly-fish, hunt, or sail. But most important, **they can talk about that which they don't do in order to engage someone who does.**

As a scientist specializing in major AIDS research at Genentech, Dr. Michael Powell says the "ability to converse is the second most important thing a scientist does to communicate what was done." In addition to traveling the world presenting papers, Mike is an adventurer. He goes scuba diving, rappelling, camping in the wilds, and flying his airplane. Mike is at ease in the tundra or in a tuxedo—or being the only man at an all-female crony dinner I attended. With his peers, Mike "avoids doing the jockeying that guys tend to do."

SIBLING REVELRY: Child ConverSensations

Some ConverSensations grew up in homes where family dinner table discussions were encouraged. Others, like my friend Pam Massarsky, head of communications for Chicago Teachers' Union, were told to "shush," because her father understandably craved quiet after a hard day of work. But Pam chose to ignore his admonition and continued to chat at the dinner table. As Pam's sixth-grade desk partner—in crime and conversation—I like to think I encouraged the expressive, interesting, laughter-laced conversations and communication skills that now benefit thousands of Chicago teachers and, ultimately, their students.

ConverSensation Lois Vieira, an administrator and teacher of the deaf/hard of hearing, credits encouragement from her siblings and mother for her conversational skills. "Mom would often comment about a situation, then turn to us and say, 'Imagine how this would make you feel if this happened to you.' We were expected to do just that, and respond."

Lois not only speaks her words, she signs them and teaches sign language to parents of the deaf/hard of hearing and other interested adults. She is a successful multi-dimensional communicator, a listener, and a thoughtful, interesting, and fun conversationalist who punctuates her comments with infectious laughter.

Sherris Goodwin, owner of a hospitality industry school, says her father's ability to look comfortable in any situation was an inspiration to her. "He always looked like he was having such fun that I emulated him."

Sandra Lipkowitz is a national shopping center and franchise consultant. As the only child of parents who moved a lot, Sandra "was always the new kid on the block or in school. Learning to converse was a survival mechanism that has flourished and enhanced my work, so I am able to talk with and put my clients at ease."

KICKING "BUTTE" IN MONTANA

At a Palm Springs meeting where I gave a keynote speech, I met a delightful woman who attributes her success in sales to her great conversational skills and to growing up in Butte, Montana.

She told me, "In Los Angeles, it's so big and I meet so many people, I can replay the four or five conversation tapes I have prepared in my mind and just do it over and over. With each different person, it's a new conversation. But growing up in Butte meant that I really had to learn to converse and to build depth into my communication because there were far fewer people and I saw them all the time. So, the conversations were more meaty and meaningful, and you have to be a good listener."

TO BE OR NOT TO BE–YOURSELF

We're often told: Be yourself, and you can't go wrong. But is that what ConverSensations do?

"Be yourself" is good advice, unless you notice that people are always excusing themselves and moving away from you. In that case, try being someone else! Assess and monitor your talk, your body language, and other non-verbal communications (like facial expression) so you can adjust "the volume."

Keep an eye on how formal, or informal, a particular situation is. While a few of the ConverSensations said they do not speak differently to peers, clients, bosses, most said that a certain *level of formality* is appropriate in business conversation and specific situations. (Appearance is also important. Being appropriately attired for the occasion can make you feel more comfortable.) In a world that often lacks civility, we can distinguish ourselves by demonstrating it.

"In your town, your reputation counts; in another, your clothes do."
—THE TALMUD
SABBUTH 1413

Most people said they "were themselves," although one ConverSensation said her irreverence was so "off the chart" that she monitored herself in certain business situations.

CONVERSENSATION DO'S

PEARLS OF WISDOM FROM
THOSE TERRIFIC TALKERS

- Honor people's time. Be bright, be brief, be gone.
- Smile and use humor.
- Tell amusing or engaging anecdotes.
- Listen, observe, study.
- Relax, share, and have faith.
- Engage in eye contact.
- Enjoy life and others will find you enjoyable.
- Remember that everyone has something to share. Conversation is fun, stimulating, and educational.
- Be courteous.

CONVERSENSATION DON'TS

WHAT THE TERRIFIC TALKERS AVOID

- Touching when talking, except when you know it's appropriate
- Giving a lot of detail in casual conversation
- Being intrusive

- Talking about touchy topics like the NRA, abortion, religion, or politics
- Encouraging people who seem weird
- Eavesdropping and butting in
- Ignoring the "space" of others
- Glancing around the room when talking to others
- Forcing yourself on people
- Telling people they are wrong

PLAN, PRACTICE, AND PREPARE

ConverSensations prepare for events. They do their homework—whether they are heading off for a board meeting, client event, or get-together with peers. Maggie Wilderotter, CEO of WINK Communications, says, "I work at keeping abreast of business challenges, our industry, and key areas of focus."

Larry Katzen, managing partner of Arthur Andersen's St. Louis office (and my senior prom date), suggests to those who want to be confident conversationalists, "Plan, prepare, and realize that what you think is the worst that can happen rarely does."

My longtime friend Carl LaMell, Executive Director of Clearbrook Center, has the gift of talking to people from all walks of life—and says he practices by talking to himself! A lot of people do. Mental rehearsal and practice help us succeed. We just have to make sure that our self-talk and mental rehearsals are all positive.

> *"No tongue speaks as much ill of us as our own."*
> —**SHOLEM ALEICHEM, 1859-1916**

MR. AND MS. MANNERS:
SOME TIPS FROM THE TOP

Think of the titans of industry, the barons and baronesses of business past and present. In spite of the informality in some workplaces today, people at the top know—and mind—their manners. They know how to converse and how to behave in polite society.

Cheryl Niggle, CEO of the Honolulu Zoological Society, believes in *the Aloha Spirit of hospitality* and says, "Politeness and kindness go a long way. Whether or not your conversation is brilliant, you will be welcome if you are sincere, caring, and treat others with dignity and respect."

Cheryl contends that her ability to converse has sky-rocketed her career and greatly contributed to her fund-raising skills. At events with clients, sponsors, volunteers, and donors, Cheryl makes sure that "they feel honored and special, like part of the *ohana* [family]."

STEPPING FORWARD, STEPPING BACK

ConverSensations have a knack for knowing when to put themselves forward, and when to step back in the dance of conversation.

John Marks, CEO of the San Francisco Convention and Visitors Bureau, advises: "Be enthusiastic, weave a good story, but don't dominate conversation."

His top tip: Learn to relate to many types of people.

At business events, Carl LaMell tries to be seen and to meet as many people as possible. "But I do not hog people's time. If they are important, other people need to meet them. They'll appreciate your being aware of that and taking the initiative to excuse yourself. You can always follow up with a note!" When he was CEO of the Victor Neumann Association, Carl took it from a half-million-dollar base to a ten-million-dollar base.

WHAT CEOS DO TO BE CONVERSENSATIONS

- Plan.
- Prepare.
- Practice.
- Don't try to sell themselves.
- Listen well.
- Ask good open-ended questions.
- Smile and be friendly.
- Focus on their conversation partners.
- Keep current.
- Articulate educated opinions.

MARS AND VENUS IN CONVERSATION

Just what do male CEOs talk about? Bill Newton says, "CEOs, the guys, talk about business and personal histories [schooling, companies, and kids]." When Bill finds out, for example, that his conversation partner is also a veteran, it establishes an immediate bond.

"But I am less interested in hearing and discussing personal accomplishments than economic policies, concepts, world events, and politics. Exchanging views, ideas, and information interests me. Yes, we do talk about activities: golf, fishing, hunting. It's a way of getting to know people via their interests. And we do compete at these activ-

41

ities. Who catches the first fish, the longest, the heaviest—it's part of the outing."

What do women CEOs have to say? Women who become CEOs are often exceptional. Robin Bacci, CEO of R.A.B. Motors, told me of her visit to "ice school," where the CEOs of automobile dealerships learn everything there is to know about driving on slick ice. The women did better than the men because "Our instructor said we paid closer attention to the instructions and followed them." Listening, learning, and being willing to follow instructions are ways to "race" to success—and women excel at these skills.

A panel of Seattle-based women CEOs addressed a national conference where I was the closing keynote speaker. They believed that *their success was enhanced by the UNDERestimations made of them by their male (and female) colleagues!* Lemonade from lemons.

FOUR BASIC CONVERSENSATION THOUGHTS FOR SUCCESS

1. Don't be impressed with yourself. We are all replaceable.
2. Stay motivated. Like what you're doing.
3. Make a commitment to follow through.
4. Communicate. Know that it is giving and receiving.

—P.J. LIVINGSTON

The words of wisdom, insights, truths, struggles, and stories of ConverSensations from all walks of life provide information, inspiration, hope, and a game plan for those who want to be confident conversationalists.

REMINDERS

- ConverSensations are "comfortable in their own skin."
- Each person credited their success with their ability to converse.
- Not one of them demeaned "small talk."
- They smile, laugh, and are lighthearted.
- Bottom line: ConverSensations like people.

CHAPTER 4

EVEN IF YOU ARE *NOT* SHY ...
READ THIS

This chapter is filled with tips for making easy, fluent conversation—whether you are shy, or whether you are eager to upgrade the equality of your already-convivial conversation!

Of the ConverSensations whom I surveyed for this book, *75 percent confessed that they either used to be shy, or are still shy.* Shyness is a common trait among extraordinary conversationalists. Clearly, it doesn't have to keep us from speaking effectively with others—for fun and profit.

The only difference between these successful, highly effective communicators and ConverSensations-in-waiting is that they have already moved through their shyness and know how to leave their conversation partners with warm, positive feelings—and the rest of us are about to do so now. Dr. Christopher McCullough, author of *Always at Ease,* refers to this as a counterphobic reaction, in which people push through their fear to overcome it.

The rewards of moving through shyness to being a ConverSensation are well worth the effort—in terms of professional success, personal satisfaction, and general well-being. This chapter is about how to make that leap of faith. It is filled with tips for making quality conversation—tips that are equally valuable for the shy and the not-so-shy.

THE SHY GUY OR GAL

If the idea of a party, trade show, fund-raiser, or meeting gives you pause or makes you uncomfortable, *you are normal!* Eighty-eight percent of the general population identify ourselves as shy in some situations. Take heart. We're in the majority, and we're in good company.

Many famous and successful people were—or are—extremely shy. Former U.S. Ambassador Sam Lewis said that the late Israeli Prime Minister Yitzhak Rabin was very shy, a quality that was often mistakenly interpreted as coldness or aloofness.

Robin Bacci, the shy CEO of R.A.B. Motors, works in a male-dominated world. She shares this secret: "It's okay to acknowledge your shyness, but also visualize yourself as an excellent conversationalist." She also suggests allowing some time alone to "recharge" after an intense social or business/social event, and always being courteous. Robin follows her own advice. I met her in a one-stall ladies' room at Saks Fifth Avenue, where she invited me to go first!

A CLASSIC AND CLASSY CASE...STUDY

My most inspiring case of "triumph over shyness" is ConverSensation P.J. Livingston, the affable, pleasant, and very well-mannered senior vice president of a major medical malpractice insurance company. P.J. is highly respected in his field, and often called upon as an industry expert for his insights and information. I met him when I gave a program for his sales staff and senior executives.

P.J. is so outgoing and verbal that you'd think he was born talking. Not so! He says that early in life he was "painfully shy and not at all a communicator." Because there was such a dramatic contrast between who he is now and who he was, I asked P.J. Livingston to be a "case study" for this book, to talk in depth about what he did to change—and how that change affected his life and contributed to his success.

P.J. is six foot three and was always tall for his age. When we met, he was in his early forties and vice president of sales and communication (one and the same, in my view). Fairly new to the San Francisco Bay Area, he had worked in Omaha and Michigan, where he had grown up as one of ten children on a farm.

P.J. feels his size had something to do with his shyness. "There are expectations of those of us who are tall and big. We had to act mature and responsible even as kids— and sometimes people felt a little intimidated or in danger because of our size. That made me self-conscious and contributed to my shyness."

Though P.J. went to a very small high school, there was a hierarchy based on social class: There were the kids of the supervisors and entrepreneurs, the kids from the mines, and then the kids from the farms. Nor did he get much attention at home. "When you're one of ten children, everyone vies for part of the attention pie and no one gets a full slice. So I just wasn't much of a talker." To P.J., shyness was "a debilitating disease abated only by a participation in sports in which size was an asset."

Fortunately, his math teacher helped him and became a "mentor who saw qualities in me I didn't know I had in myself. He gave me the role model and confidence I lacked. I made a conscious decision to change and let it be okay that I would talk to people. Because of his belief in me, his interest and attention, I wanted to emulate him."

What P.J. Livingston did (and still does) was study people. He observed the appearance, carriage, demeanor, and mannerisms of those who were comfortable and confident conversationalists. He listened to people he thought were good role models, and the people with whom they conversed.

In college, P.J. was elected president of his fraternity and to the student body governing board. "Acceptance came because I pushed through the shyness. One of the lessons I learned early on was to do things right. I didn't want anyone to think as poorly of me as I did of myself. To distinguish myself, I developed tremendous follow-through."

P.J. still battles shyness, he told me as we sat in his richly appointed office overlooking the beautiful San Francisco Bay. "Growing up on a farm, I knew I could always make a living with my hands, but I didn't want to *have* to do that. There were only two people I knew in the town who wore a white shirt: the banker and the insurance man. I aspired to wear that white shirt." By twenty-three, P.J. was the top salesperson for his company. By forty-three, he was senior vice president of sales and operations.

"I learned three big lessons from being a shy student of people:

1. Overcoming shyness is a lifetime commitment.
2. If we put people in *their* comfort zone, they communicate better. So I study, adapt, and emulate.
3. If something does not work for me the second time, I don't do it again."

The ability to converse has opened many doors for P.J. Livingston, both personally and professionally. A voracious reader who can converse on a variety of topics, he is involved with his professional organizations, in the community, with his sons' activities and teams, and in his church.

P.J. works to make others feel comfortable with him, especially people who are shorter. (Being four foot eleven, I appreciate that.) He often arrives early for meetings so he can be seated when others enter. In a stand-up conversation, he stands far enough away from his partner so as not to tower over the other person, but close enough to be heard.

The key to this ConverSensation's success, both socially and in business, is making others feel at ease. That comes naturally when we like people, and many shy people move through their discomfort because of their genuine interest in others. They are good conversationalists because we feel their interest and warmth when they look us in the eye and pay attention to what we say.

WHY NOT TO BE SHY: NANNY FINE

Imagine that it is a year from now—and you are in the position of your dreams! Everything you've ever wanted has become a reality, and it all happened because you moved beyond shyness and seized the opportunity of a lifetime. You reached out and started a conversation with the person who made your dreams come true. Sound like a fairy tale? For actor Fran Drescher (CBS's *The Nanny*), that is exactly what happened.

Fran had a unique idea for a sitcom: A Jewish woman from Flushing, complete with New York accent and *shtick*, is the nanny for three very rich, very British children.

Amazingly enough, this nanny looked and sounded just like Fran!

While sitting on a plane, waiting to take off for Paris on a ticket that had been upgraded to first class, Fran spotted Jeffrey Sagansky, a CBS entertainment executive, coming down the aisle. It seemed like a sign; she had met Jeffrey and realized that if she had the courage to speak to him, he would be a captive audience all the way across the Atlantic. "What was he going to do?" she asked. "Run away to coach? Being shy would have been easier, but the end result would have been costly. So I ran to the bathroom, put on more makeup, and said hello to him."

The rest is history. Fran Drescher's *The Nanny* is a CBS sitcom hit. Her book, *Enter Whining,* is a best-seller and she has a Nanny doll on the market. She chose to push through her inclination to be shy and, being a loyal fan, I'm grateful she didn't take the easy way out.

THE WORLD IS HER OYSTER

When Rosa Baez-Lopez was hired as a receptionist for a nonprofit in 1979, she was a quiet, shy woman with no college degree. But she had skills, worked hard, did a good job, and had a congenial manner. After a year, her boss offered her a promotion. The catch was that the new position meant expanding her role as a communicator beyond the reception area. Rose refused the new opportunity because of her shyness and lack of confidence.

Six months later, Rosa realized that she had enough confidence to go forward, so she sought the promotion that she had previously turned down. She eventually became the boss's executive assistant and worked as a team with him.

As the nonprofit's base grew from a half million dollars to ten million dollars, so did Rosa's responsibilities, skills, and confidence. Her boss was a classic mentor who knew when she was ready to move up. When he was courted and hired by another nonprofit, he recommended her as the vice president of Human Resources. The interview was tough, but Rosa knew the business and answered each question with clarity, common sense, vision, and the experience of fourteen years in the field. She got the position, and has done a spectacular job.

Is Rosa shy? "Yes, I still feel that I am shy but there is a job to do and clients to be served. We have to talk with board members, vendors, regulators, the families of our developmentally disabled clients, as well as with the businesses where our clients work. I have to be conversant with each group and each person. And I have to interview, hire, and work with each member of our staff. There is no time for my shyness."

Rosa's competence and confidence have increased her ability to converse in a multitude of situations.

SHY RECOVERY

It's in our interest to overcome shyness for both personal and professional reasons. People often perceive shy people to be aloof, disinterested, or snobbish—and that can have a disastrous impact.

There are some specific measures we can take to overcome shyness, and I offer this program of "Recovery from Shyness."

A Seven (A Bargain Reduced from Twelve) Quick-Step Shyness Recovery Program

1. **Realize that you must recover.** The ability to communicate and converse is part of the business and career milieu. Bosses expect it. If you *are* the boss, you are expected to do it.
2. **Be approachable.** Smile. Make eye contact. This is natural for shy people, who tend to focus on their conversation partners rather than scanning the room while engaged in conversation.
3. **Have three to five interesting news stories to discuss,** and read a few book or movie reviews. Better yet, read the whole book, go to the movies or theater, attend comedy clubs, join a book club, or go to the newest restaurant. (Thanks for this suggestion to Dr. Philip Zimbardo, author of *Shyness: What It Is, What to Do About It.)*
4. **Practice three to five incidents or stories that happened to you or others.** It might be something funny, provocative, or "ear-catching."
   - **Borrow people's lives.** Relate a story someone else shared about their kids, boss, vacation, or work environment. I repeat great lines from my favorite television shows.
   - **Practice saying it.** Remember that the main point, or punch line, comes last.
5. **Take an acting or improvisation class.** You'll meet other people who may be shy, and you'll learn to take risks in a safe setting.
6. **Take a conversation class** at a local college, extension, or lifelong learning center.
7. **Practice.** Smile, say hello, and talk to people along all the paths of life: the bridle path, the bike path, the track, and in the elevator. Bite the bullet, take the risk,

and say something. You'll be pleasantly surprised. People respond in kind 90 percent of the time.

In my speeches, I encourage people to talk to senior citizens. The supermarket or hardware store are good places to strike up conversations. These conversations are good "practice," good deeds, and can be fascinating. Senior browsers and shoppers have experience, stories, and good advice. Focusing on others helps us reduce our apprehension and push through our reluctance to meet and converse with others.

THREE BRIGHT IDEAS

How did those 75 percent of ConverSensations who consider themselves shy learn to work through their discomfort?

One way was *focusing on others,* as P.J. Livingston did. Another was *acting like the host,* making sure everyone was at ease, introduced, and felt welcome—as we discussed in Chapter 2.

Here is another idea: *Speak to an "important" person* (CEO, elected official, celebrity) the next time you go to an event. Don't assume that they are indifferent, snobbish, or don't want to talk to you. Statistically, they are more likely to be shy than they are to be indifferent or snobbish!

Help them out by saying something—anything. **Melt the ice** by focusing on the event. Reveal a bit of information about yourself. Remember, they had childhoods, and have kids, computers, alma maters, hobbies, interests, and favorite charities. A point worth repeating: *Conversation is part of a process that builds rapport, trust, relationship, and success.*

"Anyone who needs to be treated with deference has little to contribute to conversations," according to Norcal Insurance CEO Bill Newton.

READY OAR NOT: THREE WAYS TO BUILD CONVERSATION

There are three ways we can always contribute to the banquet of banter. The OAR Method will make sure you are never "up the creek without a paddle . . . or an OAR."

O Offer an Observation.
Example: "I thought the local critic's review of the new Harvey Keitel movie was overly judgmental. I didn't think the violence and sex were at all gratuitous. Normally, I don't like either, but it captured the essence of the underground drug world."
A Ask a Question.
Example: "Have you seen Harvey Keitel's new movie? What did you think? Would you recommend it? Was it entertaining (provocative, dramatic)?"
R Reveal Your Thoughts, Ideas, or Opinions.
Example: "I'm a great fan of Harvey Keitel, although I hated *Reservoir Dogs*. In my opinion, it *was* one. I thought *The Piano* was more memorable."

Revealing ourselves and sharing what we think, believe, feel, know, or have experienced makes a conversation deeper and more intimate. It is a *risk*, but the reward is that our well-timed revelations allow for a more meaningful exchange. Those conversations nurture and build relationships, turning contacts and strangers into associates and friends.
Warning: When offering an opinion or presenting our-

selves as knowledgeable, we must be sure we really do know what we're talking about. "Running off at the mouth" does *not* build conversation, and people may call us on our comments.

SMALL TALK TOPICS

Whether or not we are shy, it's a good idea to prepare several topics of conversation *before* we head out for the meeting, reception, or hospitality suite. There are some general subjects that you can personalize or adapt to your location:

- Sports (national and local hockey, baseball salaries, expansion teams, etc.)
- Weather (the good, the bad, and the ugly)
- Local events
- Film and art festivals, auctions, community theater
- PBS telethon
- Traffic/parking problems
- Latest movie (Academy Awards, Emmys, Golden Globes)
- Best-selling books
- Friends of the Library book sale
- Magazine articles
- Hobbies (stamp collecting, quilting, line dancing)
- Politics, politicians, scandals
- Local school district issues
- Holidays (St. Patrick's, Easter, Chinese New Year, Presidents' Day, Labor Day)
- Alma maters (from grammar school on)
- Favorite tournaments (LPGA, Masters, NCAA, Wimbledon)
- The venue

- The event (wedding, meeting, product preview, trade show, fiftieth wedding anniversary, christening, or *bris*)
- The host

ADDING TO THE ARSENAL: COLLECTING VIGNETTES

Borrow an idea from professional speakers, and develop a collection of colorful vignettes, quotes, and *bons mots* to use in conversation. Gather together these sayings and stories from published collections, or from personal experience. Our own lives, and the lives of our friends and colleagues, are full of entertaining, edifying stories.

My collection includes personal tales, magazines (*Fortune, Wired, Hemisphere, Publishers Weekly*), books, television shows (*The Nanny, Homicide: Life on the Street, Days of Our Lives*), and movies. I even keep paper with me in movies and have learned to write in the dark. More miraculously, I've learned to read what I wrote!

Don't be afraid to use "classic" stories and one-liners from years past. We are not dating ourselves; many of these classic shows and movies are still being shown. Some examples:

- When Woody Allen and Diane Keaton are crawling on the floor trying to capture the lobsters they're having for dinner in *Annie Hall,* he says to her, "You do it. You speak *shellfish.*"
- *The Golden Girls'* Estelle Getty (the eighty-plus mother whose stroke erased her verbal inhibitions), after Blanche's suave uncle overcompliments her, "To listen to this, I need boots!"
- Rhoda Morgenstern's classic line in *The Mary Tyler Moore Show,* when she looks at the piece of chocolate

in her hand and says, "Mary, I don't know why I bother putting this in my mouth. I should just apply it directly to my hips!"

Each of these comments is part of my conversational collection—and I always attribute the source. Other great lines come from Lucy and Desi, Mr. Kotter, Hawkeye Pierce, Jerry Seinfeld, Roseanne, or Nanny Fine (Fran Drescher).

When quotes are read, remembered, and repeated, they contribute to conversation. They reveal our predilections, and may strike a chord with the like-minded—as I have found often happens with Rhoda Morgenstern's "chocolate on my hips" line.

LIVING CONVERSATIONS

People who have the ability to converse easily, affably, and interestingly are *involved* in life. They are more than what they do for a living. Most of the CEOs I surveyed golf, fish, sail, read, run, ski, or do all of the above. Many play tennis, racquetball, or computer games.

They are chamber of commerce presidents, head of the United Way, or serve on their alumni board of directors. They co-chair or underwrite symphony fund-raisers, partnering projects with public schools, or corporate marathons.

They are also involved with people, and cultivate relationships. The University of Chicago Distinguished Speaker Series hired me to speak to the M.B.A. program because the recruiters realized that these brilliant people sorely lacked social skills.

I advised the students to look around the auditorium and said, "The people in this room are your network for the next fifty years. Get to know each other now. Join your alumni association and stay in touch. The 'what do I talk about' dilemma is solved. It's the university, the professors, the course work, the current standing, the campus and the favorite hangouts."

SHOES TO SCHMOOZE: SOLEFUL CONVERSATION

Overcoming shyness often means seizing the moment, and speaking about something that is right under our noses—or on our feet.

As I was writing this chapter at Spinelli's Coffee Company, I happened to glance down and spotted a great pair of shoes on a fellow customer's feet. Although I had seen her often, we had never spoken. But a great-looking pair of shoes vanquished my restraint.

"What a great pair of shoes! Where did you get them?"

Deborah Hoke-Smith regaled me with the delightful tale of her "acquisition." After that initial contact, we said hello and chatted on and off for a month before I discovered that she is a vice president of Charles Schwab and manages the local office.

Sharing a sincere compliment is one way to begin or contribute to a conversation. People love hearing that something about them is appreciated, valued, or noticed.

"Striking up a conversation" is easier when we acknowledge something that is striking.

BE A RISK-TAKER ONCE-REMOVED

It's always a relief for shy people to discover that we don't have to be Indiana Jones in order to hold up our end of the conversation.

Whenever the subject of adventures comes up, you can bet I don't have a whitewater rafting, rappelling, marathon in the Sahara, kayaking the Nile, or swimming from Africa to Europe story to share. But David Miln Smith, my Santa Cruz–based buddy, speaker, and author of *Hug the Monster*, does. So I participate by talking about him and *his* impressive adventures.

When it comes to risk-taking, I have my own style. Like many entrepreneurs, I do my thrill-seeking by reviewing income projections and accounts receivable. That can be hair-raising—and establish a common ground for conversation with other small-business people.

SHINE THE LIGHT

Memorize these questions:

- "What do you think?"
- "How did you become interested in . . . ?"
- "I am considering taking up _____ (golf, tennis, yoga, weight lifting, the Internet). Would you recommend a class or individual lessons?"

These questions highlight *someone else's* expertise and experience. Shining the light on others is a way to feel more comfortable ourselves, and one of the best ways I know to overcome shyness. It also allows us to participate, even when we are not totally prepared.

REMEDIES FOR "BETTER BANTER"

Some people are reluctant conversationalists because they're not sure about proper grammar and usage. That makes sense. Or perhaps self-consciousness about a regional or foreign accept keeps us from adding our "two cents."

If conversation is stymied for either of these reasons, we can seek out some of the many books on correct English, or classes on speaking at local colleges and resource centers. Audiotape programs with workbooks and self-paced software programs are also available.

To overcome these difficulties, I recommend three action steps:

- **Set a goal.** Learn a new word every day. I keep an unabridged dictionary open near my desk so that when I read a word I don't know, I can look it up.
- **Listen to "the well-spoken phrase."** Jot down words or phrases you especially like.
- **Take a class.** Many companies offer seminars and in-house programs for enhancing language skills. Courses are also offered at local community colleges.

When I taught in Chicago, I encouraged my students to listen carefully to the evening news. English was used correctly, verbs and subjects matched tenses, and nouns were modified by adjectives. The students developed an ear for the language, even before they could quote the rules, and learned to use English correctly in a natural way.

Improving our use of the language requires commitment, time, and effort—but it dramatically increases our comfort level and the quality of our contribution to the conversation potluck.

THE SILENT DICHOTOMY

Shy people know that silence can also contribute to the banquet of conversation—if used in moderation.

If we all talk at the same time, no one is listening. Silence gives us, and others, time to digest information, assimilate data, and assess stimuli. Speech coach Ron Arden, a former director, actor and professor of theater, coaches professional speakers and executives on the use of pausing during a presentation.

But every cliché has an equal and opposite cliché:

- "Silence Is Golden" . . . but it can also be deadly—at a performance review, a sales call, a parent-teacher conference, or a family holiday dinner.
- "The Strong, Silent Type" . . . may be weak in spirit, strength, and words.
- "Still Waters Run Deep" . . . but they can also be shallow.

"A closed mouth gathers no feet."

—UNKNOWN

"INCIDENTAL" CONVERSATION

Many great conversations, and relationships, begin as accidents or incidental events.

An interviewee noticed a woman his mother-in-law's age as he and his sons were waiting on line at a ski lift in Lake Tahoe. "I started talking to her, as my sons rolled their eyes, and discovered that she owned a second house in Tahoe which she rented to vacationers. The upshot was she rented it to our family—for half the rent we usually pay during ski season."

Whether or not we are shy, it pays to extend ourselves

to others and make them feel comfortable in conversation. It's a way to make ourselves feel more comfortable as well, and that results in good relationships and good business.

REMINDERS

- **Seventy-five percent of the ConverSensations I surveyed said they either had been shy or were still shy.**
- **Being shy is normal, but to succeed we must step out of our shell.**
- **Try the OAR approach:**
  Offer an Observation
  Ask a Question
  Reveal Your Thoughts, Ideas, or Opinions
- **Collect sayings and stories from life, television, books, movies, and friends.**
- **Compliments are great conversation starters.**
- **Shine the light on others.**
- **Even if you are shy, give it a try!**

CHAPTER 5

READING YOUR WAY TO GREAT CONVERSATION

The canvas of conversation is a collage we fill by doing our homework, and by being well-rounded, well-versed, well-read, and well-prepared.

This chapter is about the joys and benefits of reading your way to ConverSensation-hood.

READ, READ, READ

Most of the ConverSensations I surveyed attributed a great deal of their success to being well-read on a broad range of topics. They read papers, journals, industry newsletters, on-line services, and even (thank goodness!) books.

There is simply no substitute for reading a daily local and a national newspaper. "In order to be conversant, one must be well-informed. In order to be well-informed, one must be well-read," said one ConverSensation. Reading the paper lets us *contribute* to conversations in a manner that exudes comfort and confidence.

"Read" is the better part of *"ready."* A very successful partner with a prestigious Pittsburgh law firm told me that

he reads four newspapers daily. When I gave a "How to Work a Room" presentation at his firm, his colleagues identified him as a savvy socializer.

"I read the local paper, the *New York Times, Wall Street Journal,* and *USA Today* because we have clients across the country and it has comprehensive sports coverage. That way I always know the scores, and that helps me make conversation cross-country."

We are more likely to recognize someone's name or company if we are well-read. It's not important to remember *where* or even *why* we've heard of them—only that we *have.* We can start a conversation by asking something like, "Your name/company sounds familiar. Didn't I read about you recently?"

Newspapers give us information about general topics—traffic, parking problems, the weather—and also about their local applications. The weather is a great topic because everyone experiences it. If the weather has been unusual, there is double cause for conversation: the "Blizzard of '96," Denver's lack of snow, Chicago's record-breaking heat, Dallas' humidity.

Reading books and magazines outside our own profession or avocation makes us well-rounded and helps create conversation with successful people outside our field. I began subscribing to *Wired* so I could be more conversant in the computer world.

Successful conversationalists always have several current, all-purpose topics at hand from their reading that they can use as appropriate. They may even have the company librarians do research—or get on their computers and do it themselves—to be better prepared for specific events. This is something that all of us can do to be ConverSensations.

HOW TO USE THE NEWS: THE SIX KEYS

MAKING THE NEWS WORK FOR YOU . . .

1. **Peruse** the capsule column of the newspaper for highlights.
2. **Scan** the front page, reviewing the headlines of each story.
3. **Read** the first paragraph of each interesting or relevant story. Journalists still give the "who, what, where, when, why and how" summary in the first paragraph.
4. **Determine** if the article is of interest or important to you—or your clients.
5. **Review** each section of the paper. It's just as important to know the cultural news in your city as it is to know the metro news, sports, or business. Your clients or potential clients may be just as likely to underwrite a Leukemia Society benefit or a ballet performance as they are to sponsor a tennis match, golf tournament, or 10K race. You may decide to buy a seat or table, or to send a contribution or note of acknowledgment, or good wishes for success.
6. **Avoid reading** the local paper for national or world news if you do the same in the *Wall Street Journal* or elsewhere. It's redundant.

TURNING NEWS INTO SCHMOOZE

You've "read" the newspaper. You have a sense of world, national, and local events; sports; business (current mergers, NASDAQ); entertainment, including the hottest stand-up comedy acts; and local and national weather.

How can you put all this information to work for you? Here are a few leading questions that ease news into schmooze:

- "How did you fare with your snowstorms?"
- "Did the floods affect you?"
- "How long did it take you to shovel out from the blizzard?"
- "Are you staying warm?"
- "Have you been following the trial?"
- "Did you catch yesterday's game? What a tense one—double overtime."
- "Any predictions on the World Series?"
- "Isn't it amazing that the voters decided to turn Alcatraz into a casino!"
- "How do you like those (fill in your/their hometown team)?"
- "Are you a (fill in the blank) fan?"
- "Is this your first national convention?"
- "Any thoughts on the Time Warner–Turner deal? Who do you think gets custody of the colorization discussions? Jane Fonda?"
- "Are you much of a moviegoer?"
- "Have you seen the Ingrid Bergman retrospective at the Metro?"
- "How did you get interested in Literacy Volunteers?"
- "Do you do much fishing? Favorite spot? Fly-fishing? Steelhead? Trout? Do you do your own smoking?" (Salmon, not cigarettes!)

An appropriate follow-up to many of these questions is "What did you think?"

When you are well-read, you can converse intelligently even on subjects with which you have little experience. I haven't fished since I was twelve—and I threw that one back—but I can still participate in a conversation about fishing if I've read the sports pages and kept current. All I need is a working knowledge of the subject, and enough familiarity with a topic to share information gleaned from others, or to ask good questions that keep the conversation open.

CLIPPED CONVERSATION

It is rumored that the need to read a paper or magazine with a scissors in hand is determined by a DNA configuration known as the C.S.G. (Clipping Service Gene). It was discovered at the University of Illinois in the early 1960s by a group of sorority sisters (mine) who competed to see whose anguished parents had sent them the most Ann Landers and Dear Abby columns complaining that their daughters hardly ever wrote home.

The C.S.G. is not linked to gender, and it can be either recessive or dominant. Good news for those who don't have this genetic predilection: It can be an acquired trait that contributes to our business and social success.

CLIP, SAVE, AND REREAD: HOW TO AVOID "CAN'T REMEMBER WHERE'S"

How many times have we said, "I read about that somewhere—can't remember where." I grew up with this phrase, and thought "Can't Remember Where" was the name of a prominent research journal because my mother was always quoting from it to prove her point! Now I, too, often quote from "Can't Remember Where."

One way to remember a key point or an interesting article is to read it, cut it out, file or pile it, and *reread it later.* Be sure to date the article and note its source.

CLIP AND MAIL

We can create and nurture relationships by sending articles of import or interest to those we meet or who are featured in the story. A simple Post-it™ or brief handwritten note is all that need accompany the clipping. The note might say:

- "FYI. Thought of you."
- "Congratulations on the award. Continued success."
- "Thought you might like an extra copy for the family."

Is this conversation? It certainly is. It is another piece of communication that conveys a message. The message is, "I listened to you, I remembered you, and I think highly enough of you to take the time to clip this item, add a note, and mail it to you."

GREAT LENO (HEAD)LINES

Jay Leno collects odd headlines—both for *The Tonight Show* and for his books. If we see an odd headline, we can clip it. Some of the best content for conversation comes from those odd filler items.

In my speeches, I give examples of great headlines and

stories that contribute to conversation, like, "I saw the funniest headline . . . Did you read about the two criminal klutzes who shot each other during a robbery?" (*San Francisco Chronicle*, March, 1996)

Here are some examples of eye-catching headlines that are great conversation starters:

- "Cleaning House Can Make You Sick!" (Whoa! That's a surprise!) (*Marin County Independent Journal*)
- "Amish Woman . . . with 9 Children Live in Intercourse, PA" (Naturally!) (*Wall Street Journal*)
- "Unusual Sources of Dietary Fiber. A Snickers Bar Has More Fiber Than a Nature Valley Granola Bar." (Yeah!) (*San Francisco Chronicle*)

SPORTIN' LIFE

Women need to read the sports pages because both men and women discuss sports, teams, and scores. (And men ought to read the Lifestyle pages, which give information about the community, movies, books, arts, and culture.)

We may not play golf or tennis, but we should know something of those worlds. They provide news that is part of our culture. Everyone should be able to join a conversation about a local team, the playoffs, the World Series, or the Super Bowl.

"CUB FAN"NING THE FLAME OF CONVERSATION

Sharing "fanship," or even friendly rivalry, about sports can build conversation. This exchange took place at a business meeting:

JJ: "How do you face customer rejection?"

DS: "Being a Cubs fan does prepare one for facing rejection and disappointment."

JJ: "Do you get to many games?"

DS: "I spend a lot of time in the right field bleachers at Wrigley. It's a sweetheart of a park."

JJ: "The night lights created such controversy. How did you stand it?"

DS: "That's one change I can't make, so I don't go to night games. The night lights are a problem because, unlike most stadiums, Wrigley is right in the middle of a neighborhood. But the dollar ruled; baseball is a business. To me it's a sport. You have a favorite team?"

JJ: "I am a Dodgers fan. My dad lived in Brooklyn and always told me the stories of the games in his 'good old days.' It's not easy to be a Dodgers fan in Kansas City."

Both JJ and DS built the conversation by listening and making appropriate responses that developed rapport.

COMIC RELIEF

True confessions. I read the comics first, starting with the most profound—*Calvin & Hobbes,* whom I miss. Then there are *Bizarro, Suburban Cowgirls, Rhymes with Orange,* and *The Fusco Brothers.* Some of the best find their way into my conversation.

Sending cartoons to colleagues, clients, and friends is a great way to use the fax machine. I often add a sentence like:

- "Thought I'd send a smile."
- "Share a laugh."
- "Didn't know whether or not you've seen this."

Yes, it takes time, and we are all busy, but it contributes to the ongoing conversation of life by saying, "I paid attention to you and your interests." That makes a positive statement about both you and the other person's M.P. (memorable presence).

ADDITIONAL MATERIAL FOR MINGLING

Most professional associations produce magazines, journals, and newsletters. They are chock-full of industry issues, concerns, and information—and also provide the names of officers, movers, and shakers.

We don't have to memorize what's in these publications, only familiarize ourselves with them and the kind of information they provide, so we can look up what we need to know—when we need to know it.

If we find an article that "strikes a chord," we can send a note to the writer and/or the editor. If we have something to add or a different take on the issue, we can offer to write an article—a point-counterpoint piece.

If someone asks if you've read a particular article in one of these journals and you have *not*, tell the truth and inquire, "What did it say?" **Then listen to the summary and comment on it, building a conversation.**

TECHNO-SCHMOOZE

Reading the business pages, news, and Lifestyle sections of newspapers and magazines provides great material on technology. Today, these are only a few of the subjects with which we need to be familiar.

If the person to whom we are speaking is not a computer user, there is still a conversation. We can share our progress from computer illiterate to computer convert. At a recent sorority reunion, eight of the sorors were discussing the benefits of e-mail and two of us who communicated on-line persuaded others to join us in bicoastal conversations. There I was, the recovering computerphobe, explaining how to do e-mail by flash session!

We know techno savvy is part of the "pop cultcha" when television series, dramas, and comedies feature e-mail as part of solving a mystery or sending a romantic message to the wrong person.

And it is here to stay. Learn, discuss, and do!

There is no substitute for being well-informed, and the best way to do that is to read, read, read.

REMINDERS

- **Prepare for conversation by reading newspapers, magazines, journals, and books.**
- **Turning news into schmooze is a five-step process: Read, Clip, File or Pile, Reread, and Repeat.**
- **To know the score, read the sports section.**
- **C.S.G.—Clipping Service Gene—forces us to read with a scissors and mail our clippings.**
- **Collect favorite quotes to contribute to conversation.**
- **For comic relief, read the comics.**

CHAPTER 6

HEAR, HEAR—LEND ME YOUR EAR

The secret of being a great conversationalist?

L - I - S - T - E - N.

We all have to bring something to the conversation potluck, but we also have to listen. Tasting and appreciating what others have brought to the banquet is easy, fun, and informative. It gives us something to which we can respond, and that's called conversation.

Every survey I've taken indicates that the best conversationalists are wonderful listeners. People want to converse, and do business, with those who listen. No one goes around saying, "I really like my doctor (accountant, mechanic, computer consultant). You ought to use him. He doesn't listen to me!"

When we are quiet for a moment, when we smile, nod, and focus our eyes and attention on the person who is talking, he or she knows that we are listening—if we really *are* listening—and not just pretending to do so.

OFF IN SPACE

We've all traveled off to some secret place during a sermon, a ceremony, a meeting, or with a less-than-engaging speaker—and we can usually tell when someone else drifts off on *us*. My thirteen years as an educator prepared me to identify the dreamers, the drifters, and the dozers for whom snoring is the obvious signal. (Little did I know then that these kids were our future entrepreneurs, inventors, risk-takers, and CEOs.)

But when we "travel off" during business meetings and conversations with colleagues, would-be clients, co-workers, and bosses—not to mention loved ones—the cost may be high.

A HAIR-RAISING EXPERIENCE

My stylist Jerome Castillo hired an apprentice in his salon. "Every time I talk to her," he told me, "whether it's general conversation or explaining a procedure, she looks as if she's totally disinterested. The first few times this happened, I thought maybe she was just shy, but that's not the case. She always responds energetically, but her answers never have a shred of relevance to my comments. She's just *not listening.*"

Jerome is an easygoing boss, but when I asked him how he was coping, he said, "Susan, I'm at the end of my rope. *Our business is based on listening to customers.* If we don't pay attention to what hairstyle, cut, or color they want, their hairdo becomes a 'hair don't' and we lose a customer!"

All business is based on listening. Whether it's the local beauty salon, paper company, surgeon's office, software design firm, dry cleaner, or data processing business, listening is crucial to carrying on conversation—and conversation is how we communicate.

In business, the real waste of time is *not* listening—and not listening is also a form of communication. Beth was communicating very clearly with Jerome! She was saying, "I don't care what you have to say." That's not a productive communication to a boss, and it didn't help Beth's career.

Jerome and Beth's situation is multiplied a thousandfold across America every day—to the detriment of those who haven't learned to listen.

THE FAUX LISTENERS

My friend Claudia Jarrett once engaged a jazz musician in conversation at a party we attended. She was talking, laughing, posing questions, and relating stories. He nodded, laughed at intervals, smiled, and added a few "Really's," "You're kidding's," and "You don't say's!"

Claudia later told me, "'Mr. Musician' is quite a charming conversationalist!" I was flabbergasted. He did no work, and was just mimicking "active listening" behaviors while listening to "Take Five" in his head! How did I confirm this? I mentioned her compliment to him, and asked what the conversation had been about. He didn't know!

"Assuming the position" of listening without actually doing so can backfire. Here's a test you can use to tell whether or not someone is listening: Ask a question based on information to which the person has just agreed to, nodded, or spoken of favorably.

It is just as easy to listen as it is just to give the impression that we are listening! Both require work—but when we really listen, there is a positive payoff.

POSITIVE PAYOFFS

It's good manners and good business to listen. It's also *interesting*. It's more fun to be engaged in what another person is saying than to waste time counting the minutes until we can escape, drifting off while trying to appear to be awake, or staring at the wall.

When we truly listen, we are more likely to remember what we hear. Remembering what people have said is crucial to keeping a conversation alive. How can we respond intelligently to a comment if we are playing music or reliving past events in our head?

Listening helps us learn what we need to know about that person and his or her business.

LISTENING HER WAY TO SALES SUCCESS

Jean Miller is a former public school librarian who has become extremely successful selling a big-ticket item— library systems for public and university libraries. Jean is a very conservative, no-nonsense businessperson—and she is at the top of her field. She recently learned that she has won $6,000 in a company sales contest, on top of her commission, even though her territory had been cut in half!

Jean's secret is simple. "I ask questions, and then I keep quiet and *listen to the answers.* That's how I get the information I need to recommend solutions for the cus-tomer's requirements, and I don't sell them more than they need. People want to buy, not to be sold. A lot of salespeople are so busy selling, they just don't know when to be quiet and listen!"

"Listen to the answers" sounds easy, but many of us don't do it for one reason or another.

77

Jean has built a reputation in the industry for being a good researcher, organizer, follow-up person, and a good listener who knows how and when to use the most effective listening tool: silence.

LEADERS LISTEN

Corporate and entrepreneurial America cannot afford people who don't or won't listen. From Victor Kiam to Bill Clinton, successful leaders have to be attuned to the market, the consumer, the staff, and the client.

Listening creates conversation, conversation creates communication, and communication creates connection. When we aren't listening effectively, intelligent conversation comes to a dead halt. Remember, people want to do business with people they know, like, and trust . . . people with whom they are comfortable.

People who listen to us make us feel comfortable with them. They will always have the competitive edge not only because we know, like and trust them more, but because they are always learning and gathering information that lets them serve us, relate to us, and sell to us better.

STOP, LOOK, LISTEN

Listening is hard work that makes demands on the mind and body. Dr. Ralph Nichols, a pioneer in the field of listening research, says, "When an individual is listening, the heart rate increases, breathing rate increases, and muscles tense. A tired, stressed body that clamors for attention interferes with the ability to communicate" (Diane Corley Schnapp, "Executive Secrets," United Airlines *Hemisphere* magazine, March 1993, p. 29).

To listen well, we need to pay attention. We need to stop and look before we listen.

Stop

Effective listeners prepare by *focusing* physically and mentally. They stop other activities and pay attention to their conversation partner.

Look

Paying attention includes eye contact. It is very difficult to listen to someone when we are examining our desks, bookshelves, or golf clubs, cooking dinner, washing the car, or taking phone calls. When we aren't looking at the other person, he or she is never sure if we're listening.

As part of my presentations, I invite audience members to get up, meet, and converse with one another—whether there are sixty of them, or sixteen hundred. That's why they hire me to speak. They want people to know how to converse and make contacts. When we talk about the exercise, people always say that it feels great to be approached by another person because someone has "noticed and paid attention" to them.

They also say that what makes the conversations work is eye contact. It is off-putting to be talking to someone who is inspecting the walls, the ceiling, or the other participants. The message is, "Almost anything in this room is more interesting, attractive, and important than you are. You are chopped liver."

When people do make eye contact, they charm those with whom they speak. Are these people who "notice and pay attention" to us with eye contact the ones we remember? Want to talk to? Hire? Do business with? Refer our pals and colleagues to? Of course they are!

Listen

When we have stopped and really looked at the other person, we can listen with our ears, eyes, faces, hearts, minds, bodies, and souls.

THE CLASSIC CONVERSATION

Let's see how these listening principles work in real conversations. It begins with paying attention, being open, making eye contact, and body language that invites people in.

My friends David Schultz and Carl LaMell could have shared a classic first conversation, partly because Carl uses the miraculous technique of RESPONDING IN KIND, and both of them LISTEN. Their opening lines:

"Hello, I am David Schultz, a fanatic Cubs fan . . . and an attorney."

"Hi, I'm Carl LaMell, a devoted Sox fan and Executive Director of the Clearbrook Center."

Because David revealed his preference in baseball teams as part of an open, inviting introduction, Carl could respond in kind. A conversation on standings, stats, trades, parks (Comiskey Park vs. Wrigley Field), night games vs. day games, the "good old days," and bleachers vs. boxes can ensue.

Carl: "David, you are fanatic, well-informed, and quite supportive of the Cubs. Do you do any legal work for them?"

David: "I only wish. My clients range from people seeking divorces, personal injury cases, and several not-for-profit associations. Oh! Does the Clearbrook Center have representation?"

Carl: "Funny you should ask. Our counsel has been with us awhile and he's getting ready to retire. Do you have a card?"

David: "Right here next to my baseball card." (David takes out his card case and hands Carl two cards—one for his firm and the other of David in his Cubs uniform, No. 7, taken at Fantasy Camp.)

David and Carl's conversation reflected their *listening skills.* And they could do business together because David added a bit of fun to his self-introduction, and Carl listened and responded in kind. They "threw out bait" to which the other could "hook" their conversation.

"It takes a great man to make a 'good listener.'"
—ARTHUR HELPS

HOW DO THEY KNOW WE ARE LISTENING?

The true quality of our listening is intangible, but these two tips not only help us listen—they help *others* know that we are listening:

Nodding On—Not Off

Successful people tell me that the person who nods when being spoken to encourages conversation. Nodding shows agreement, and we always want to converse with people who encourage and agree with us.

Asking Questions

The person who asks a question about the topic under discussion, or shares a story on the subject, is an active listener. That person makes it easy to converse because he or she is "in the moment," paying attention—and creating a memorable presence because of it!

Business is always better served by those who listen actively and pay attention. Why waste our time either ignoring others or being ignored?

LISTENING PROS

We can learn a lot from professional listeners—therapists and such unofficial counselors as hairstylists, barbers, bartenders, and manicurists.

We pay these professionals partly to pay attention to us. If they're good at their jobs, they know how to make us feel heard. And talking to them often helps us hear *ourselves*. We can learn something from these folks, who often engage us with:

PROFESSIONAL LISTENING TOOLS

- Eye contact
- Slight nodding
- Focus on us and our words
- Questions and comments
- Hearing even what we don't say!

We know from our own experience that we are more open and informative when we're around people who listen. That's a good thing to remember when we want people to be open and informative around *us*—when we want to learn what's going on in a company, for instance, or what's happening with the competition, or in a certain industry.

"GET REAL" LISTENING

Part of good listening is not negating, denying, or putting down the other person's experience. *It's important to recognize and acknowledge the speaker's feelings or state of mind,* regardless of the content of his or her message.

We know how important this is with children. Sometimes when a child falls down, scrapes a knee, and starts crying, we'll say, "That didn't hurt. You're a big boy (or girl)." The truth is that the child is crying because something about the experience *was* scary and/or painful.

The appropriate response is, "Oh, you scraped your knees. That must hurt. Would you like me to wash it off and put a bandage on it?" As anyone who has kids—or once was one—knows, this must be said with empathy. Often, the crying stops simply because positive attention and a solution are offered.

As adults, we still have this "Get real!" reaction when someone tries to deny our experience or reality. We don't want our feelings to be negated, even when we may permit our facts or information to be questioned.

I learned this lesson firsthand during the 1979 layoffs of 1,200 San Francisco teachers. Many of us really loved teaching, felt as if our commitment to the (low-paying) job was being mocked, and were afraid to think about embarking on new careers. Far too many of us believed George Bernard Shaw's old saw that "He who can, does. He who cannot, teaches."

I made light of the issue, as is my way. When friends called bemoaning their fate, I came off like Susie Sunshine cheering up the troops. It didn't work—and altered a few friendships because I didn't hear people, "get real" with them, and acknowledge that their feelings were valid even though they were different from mine.

The good news is that I paid attention to the problem and my failed attempts to cheer people up. That year, I designed a career change workshop to help teachers make professional transitions.

SUSPENSION OF JUDGMENT

The first cousin to hearing and acknowledging people's experience as real (even when their facts may be questionable) is suspending judgment.

"Why did you do *that?*" is not usually what people are looking for when they relate an incident to us, perhaps an incident that's somewhat difficult to talk about. It's a real conversation stopper.

"Why would you think *that?*" and its ilk produce the same result—or else move the conversation into an adversarial mode as the other person reacts defensively to our challenge.

Setting aside judgment allows us to listen better because our effort and energy is focused on *hearing what is being said,* not on formulating our opinion or evaluation of it. Minister and counselor Sherwood Cummins says, "To ask 'Why' conveys a judgment. Asking 'How come?' is curiosity and engenders conversation."

THE ECHO MUST GO, OR "THE PERILS OF PARROTING"

Teachers and supporters of active listening have told us for years that, to clarify what people said, we should rephrase what we heard. "Did I understand you to say that . . . ?"

The result? Every conversation takes twice as long! That's hard on us Type As.

"Reframing" people's statement can be a good active listening skill, but constantly rephrasing what people say can be irritating, and even be perceived as a put-down. Worse, we can start to sound parrotlike, according to Dr. Deborah Tannen, author of several books on communication, including *You Just Don't Understand.* All of these things hinder conversation, rather than help it.

Rephrasing is one way to make sure we understood a comment, or the context in which a term is used—but there are alternatives. If we're not sure we're tracking with the speaker, we can give him or her a quizzical look, or say, "I'm unfamiliar with the term." We can even ask, "What do you mean?"

It takes a healthy ego to admit that we aren't following along, but making this clear gives our conversation partner a chance to explain or respond.

"The mockingbird effect" is the first cousin of parroting. In *The Secret Language of Success,* David Lewis writes that friends *spontaneously* and *unconsciously* mirror one another's movements. While people can deliberately copy another's stance and movements to develop empathy, he cautions us to watch out for "mimicking of movements." If we see that someone is mimicking us deliberately, we should do a sincerity check before giving them our complete trust. And we should be aware that others may be checking our sincerity.

THE GRAIN OF SALT

Experts in listening and communication can offer valuable ideas, but we have to measure each piece of advice against our own experience and circumstances—taking what works and leaving the rest.

I learned this many moons ago, when a fancy professor from a Washington university visited the elementary school where I taught. He was there to teach us "dialoging" as a way of enhancing our disciplining skills. I asked him what one does with the other twenty-nine children while this dialogue takes place with the troublemaker. "They will be listening and appreciating the process," he said with a straight face. This guy had been out of the classroom too long.

DISRUPTIVE INTERRUPTIONS

Silence is the Golden Rule of listening. Nobody likes to be interrupted, and keeping quiet also allows us to process the information we're getting—and to learn from it.

Nothing makes us lose our train of thought more quickly than being interrupted. It happens to all of us, and it is irritating. I have a colleague who is also a good pal, but he constantly interrupts me. After more times than I care to remember, I erupted, "Stop interrupting me and let me finish my sentence!" Periodically, he needs to be reminded.

Interruptions impact all conversations, but the costs may be higher in business conversations—and men are more at risk than women in this area. Research shows that men are responsible for 96 percent of interruptions in cross-sex social conversations (*San Francisco Chronicle,* February 3, 1985, based on scientific sociological research at the University of California, Berkeley, by Candace West and Don Zimmerman). That's not particularly pleasant for women. When the pattern continues in cross-sex *business* conversations, it can be devastating to the man's career. A woman in the executive suite won't take kindly to this pattern. If she is your boss, co-worker, client, or customer, the results can be disastrous.

"Never miss a good chance to shut up."
—SCOTT BEACH'S GRANDFATHER

A REGIONAL "DIS"CLAIMER

Interruptions aren't always interruptions, I discovered watching Dr. Deborah Tannen promote *That's Not What I Meant* on the *Today* show. And interruptions don't always mean that people aren't listening.

People from different geographic regions and ethnicities have different paces and patterns of communications. Someone from New York isn't necessarily interrupting when he or she interjects a loud "Wow! That's great!" It's just a form of encouragement and appreciation for the speaker's story. But if the listener is from the Midwest or South, that outburst might be considered an interruption.

When I recognized these differences, I finally understood what my then-spouse and I had done for years. I am a wildly enthusiastic, appreciative congratulator. When he would come home and tell me that his band (he was a high school music teacher and musician) had won a contest, I enthusiastically congratulated him. "That's great!" would roll right off my tongue.

"Stop interrupting me," was always his response—and it always baffled me. Although I'm from Chicago (the fast-talking part of the city), my communication pattern is strictly New York. He is from Virginia. I rest my case.

LISTENING TO OURSELVES

Some people talk and talk and talk. They rarely hear other people—and even worse, they don't hear themselves. Part of speaking is listening to ourselves—and to our listeners' reactions to us.

An associate told me about a meeting he attended with a business partner, attorneys, and a client. "George never shut up. He must have thought we were all there to listen to his soliloquy. He's no Hamlet; just a plain ham. Moreover, he blew the deal. I realize he was nervous and thought he had to fill in the blanks, but *he* never heard a word he said."

If the voice we hear most often in conversation is our own, it's time to reassess. If we think we are so brilliant, so amusing, or so articulate that people can't stop listening to us, we may not be attuned to the group—whether we are at a meeting, dinner party, or business lunch or dinner. It's not enough to be a great storyteller; we must also be aware of others and direct the conversation so as to include them.

Silence can be golden for speakers, as well as for listeners. It is the pause that refreshes. Appropriately placed pauses allow others to "chime in" without feeling that they are interrupting.

As we listen to ourselves, we should remember that people generally prefer to converse with those who bring energy, enthusiasm, animation, or joie de vivre to the conversation. It's appropriate to take what we do seriously, but we can't take it *too* seriously. In other words, we may need to en"light"en up.

If we feel that the response we are getting to our communication and presence is not as positive as we would like, a class in spontaneity, listening skills, impromptu acting, or humor might be a good investment. Courses that provide video feedback give us a firsthand experience of how we look and come across to others when we are conversing. A good coach or teacher can also help.

We can also use the "birds of a feather" approach: Hang out with animated, interesting, confident conversationalists who listen to themselves and others.

LISTENING TO THE BORING

How do we listen to the slow, serious, unexpressive, or boring communicator—especially when we don't have a choice because that person is our boss, or the client who is considering the half-million-dollar hardware system we are selling?

I'm reminded of sitting in a college lecture hall with a boring professor who droned on and on—but he was the one giving the tests and the grades! He held all the cards, so I listened, took notes, and got past his style.

Sometimes the way we listen can actually make people speak in a more interesting or enthusiastic way. *People often get more animated when conversing about those things for which they have passion.* If we can pinpoint an area of expertise or interest, the person may come to life and become a scintillating conversationalist. This method isn't surefire, of course, but it works often enough that it's worth trying.

On a recent speaking engagement in Georgia, I was chauffeured by one of the company's employees to and from my presentation. He was very polite, in the old Southern style—and after twenty-six years in California, that was a nice change for me. But he was very low-key until I mentioned that I'd discovered (by "working the room" at the presentation) that my hotel had an arrangement with a local health club that had free weights, and that I worked out with a personal trainer using the free weights, not machines. Little did I know that he was into strength training, too! He lit up as he talked about his club and routine. He told me his preferences and asked me questions about mine. He began talking faster and became more animated because he was passionate about his interest in physical fitness . . . and being buff.

BORE NO MORE

TIPS FOR LISTENING TO MR. OR MS. BORE

1. Adjust your attitude. If the conversation is about business, consider it the "cost of doing business."
2. Remember that the information may be important, even when people don't speak with animation or even move their face muscles.
3. By listening and asking questions, you may discover a special interest or avocation where you can focus the conversation—and they may come alive!

MAGIC REVISITED

Listening is magic. And it can do wonders for our confidence, conversations, and bottom line. On a PBS special memorializing the late actress Audrey Hepburn, one of her colleagues said, "She had a wonderful quality that made her different—she *listened.*"

It's a lesson we can learn from a truly gracious woman, a gem who truly did have *Breakfast at Tiffany's!*

REMINDERS

- **Good listeners are perceived as good conversationalists.**
- **Faux listeners who only look as if they're listening risk being found out.**
- **Active listening is work, but it has a huge payoff both personally and professionally.**
- **Not listening can impact our careers, jobs, and the perceptions others have of us.**
- **People do business with people they know, like, and trust—and with whom they are comfortable.**
- **People are comfortable with other people who make easy conversation and *who listen to them.***
- **Active listening includes eye contact, focusing on the other person, paying attention, responding in kind, and asking questions that relate to the comment just made.**
- **Interrupters are not appreciated. Men do it more than women, and should be conscious of this issue.**
- **Parroting may be perceived as a put-down, but clarification is critical to conversation.**

CHAPTER 7

SURELY YOU JEST!

A good sense of humor isn't always about telling the best stories or delivering the funniest punch lines. It may be the ability to *hear* humor, the gift of an infectious laugh, or the ability to find the richness of what is funny in everyday situations. All these things are wonderful contributions to conversation.

Humor is healing and revealing. In business, it can also enhance negotiations, presentations, and conversations. Having an array of anecdotes, and the willingness to share them can make us more effective mediators, communicators, and managers. Humor makes our presence more powerful.

A shared sense of humor can be a tremendous bond. Career consultant and author Marilyn Moats Kennedy suggests that it is the core ingredient in a good mentor (femtor)/protégé duo. It can also help break the ice and communicate our values.

> *"Seriousness is the only refuge of the shallow."*
> —OSCAR WILDE

WHERE DOES HUMOR LIVE?

Some of the best humor comes from everyday situations and events to which everyone can relate. These common chords always move the conversation along.

My best material comes from friends, clients, and cronies. They say funny things. Maybe they take more risks because they know I'll laugh. I take more because they do. One of the nicest compliments I ever received was from a consultant and psychologist friend who told me she never thought she was funny until she met me.

Humor lives all around us, and especially in us. It's an attitude, a combination of being good-natured and open to possibilities.

OVER-HEAR, OVER-HEAR

One good way to catch the humor around us is to "prick up our ears." My "over-hearing" is one of my best senses—and I have the good sense to use it.

I overheard a petite woman complain to a chum that she needed to lose weight. Her friend said, "Are you kidding? You're as big as a minute."

Ms. Petite's response: "The problem is that my clothes are altered for forty-five seconds!"

At an evening game at the Oakland Coliseum, a man turned to his friend and said, "This ballpark has everything—pizza, fried chicken, even sushi!" The skeptical companion said, "Believe me, when I want to go out for sushi, I don't go to the Oakland Coliseum!"

While waiting in line at the San Francisco airport, I watched as a well-dressed gentleman kept on setting off the metal detector. After a near Gypsy Rose Lee–style strip, he put his keys back in his pocket, put his belt back on, and joined his two friends as they sprinted for their plane. One man asked him what seemed to be the problem. "The penile implants do it every time." His two colleagues gulped.

I looked him in the eye, smiled, and said, "Thanks. That's going in my next book!"

His response: "I'm thrilled you don't know my last name!"

I don't know if he really had the operation, but I do know he has a sense of humor!

"FREE" WEIGHTS AND OTHER LIFE ADVENTURES

Our own lives provide a constant source for humor, if we keep our eyes and ears open.

I work out with free weights (five- and ten-pound dumbbells—those thirty-year reunions can be so motivating), and do the best I can to maintain my routine while on the road. Before leaving for a trip to Dallas, I called to ask if the hotel had free weights in their fitness facility. They told me, "Of course!" But when I arrived, I saw that they only had machines. The manager apologized for the misunderstanding and explained, "Our reservations trainee doesn't work out, and she thought the weights were free because *we don't charge a fee to use them!*"

And in the category of "new wrinkles" . . . Several years ago I noticed a deep frown line in my forehead. I called my dear friend Mumsy (Joyce) Siegel and said, "Mums, as soon as the house sells, I am going to take five hundred dollars and have a collagen shot in my forehead frown line."

"They only last six months," replied Mumsy. "Don't get one." I became quite cool, thinking she was going to tell

95

me I was perfect as I was. She continued, "Instead, save your money, and in a year and a half, have your *whole forehead lifted!*" Oh, well.

As we get older, our bodies can become a great source of gentle humor. (We can either laugh or cry.) Diane Parente is an image consultant, author, speaker, and a dear friend. She has cleaned out my closets, ridding me of anything and everything that didn't make the grade. After a shopping adventure in Scottsdale, I came home with an elegant black and silver St. John knit dress, which I tried on for her. As I looked in the mirror, I was struck with horror! I could see a bulge in my thighs. *Oy vay!*

"Parente, I swear they were not there in Scottsdale. The dress fit perfectly. The store must have had *trick* mirrors!"

"Susan, don't worry," she replied. "What will take care of that thigh problem is control-top pantyhose."

I dejectedly responded, "Parente, I am *already wearing a pair!*"

When the *San Francisco Chronicle* ran a story titled "New Cream Shrinks Women's Thighs," my friend Lana Teplick, a Boston CPA, said, "One question. How does the cream *know* it's on your thighs? If you apply it with your fingers, do they get smaller?"

IMPRESSIONIST IMPRESSIONS: LETTING OTHERS SHINE

At a Monet exhibit in San Francisco's de Young Museum, there were only three of the twenty-two paintings that I actually liked and could "see." My host was my friend Jean Miller, to whom I confided, "Jeanie, I only like three paintings. The rest seem so blurred and murky. Which of Monet's periods do you think they are from?"

Without missing a beat, Jeanie replied, "From the period when he was going blind!" I have told this true story to at least twenty acquaintances, cronies, and colleagues—and from the stage to 1,200 "Peak Performers."

Patricia Fripp, first woman president of the National Speakers Association, cautions, "We can't be the heroes of all our stories." Jeanie has the punch line in this one! And it opens up a conversation on art, preferences, artists, museums, exhibits, and other related topics. If someone doesn't want to talk about art, it can lead to a discussion of "losing sight"—the bifocal version.

JEST, DON'T FORGET

Part of humor is the ability to *see* life's quirks and ironies. Another part is *remembering* these funny moments.

Jeanne Robertson, an outstanding professional speaker and humorist from North Carolina, shares tips for capturing the humor of everyday life in *Humor: The Magic of Genie.* She suggests that we identify our daily routines and ask ourselves "What is funny about that?"

Another way to note the humor in everyday life, Robinson offers, is to subject the various tasks on our to-do list to the "Wouldn't it be funny if . . . ?" question—and then exaggerate the situation.

Her most important tip is to *write it down.* Like dreams we're sure we'll remember in the morning, these funny moments are forgotten if we don't commit them to paper (or disk). Jeanne keeps a "humor journal" of everyday occurrences so she doesn't forget experiences that turn into the wonderful stories for which she is known. (If you're a talker and not a writer, carry a cassette recorder to save these funny lines.)

I am not a joke teller, but my skill has improved

because of the "Three Wise Men" in my life. Carl LaMell, Sherwood Cummins, and Michael LeBoeuf all tell or e-mail me the new (or new to me) jokes. I always tell the other two guys and reference the source. But I have to *write down the setup and the punch line* or they are forgotten.

Collect those funny lines and stories, and repeat them to your friends and family. If they respond positively, the anecdotes are keepers to refine and possibly share in business conversations. Remember, the punch is always the last line.

PUT DOWN THE PUT-DOWNS

The use of disparaging humor—ethnic, racial, gender, or sexual jokes—is never appropriate. These put-downs and off-color comments are less common today because we're more aware of sexual harassment, diversity is increasing in the workplace, and we've become more sensitive to the negative reactions that this type of humor creates.

Always avoid humor that happens at the expense of others. One person's funny joke is another person's conversation killer. Questionable jokes are not worth the risk. There is enough humorous material in the world, and in our daily lives, that we don't have to put down anyone or any group to get a cheap laugh.

Be especially careful about repeating jokes in business conversations. If the purpose of business conversation is to establish connection, communication, and rapport, then we want our humor to support that purpose—*not subvert it.*

THE ETHNIC ETHOS

While we do have to be sensitive about put-downs, we don't have to avoid our ethnic and regional roots. Sometimes we can even use them to our advantage, if we're careful.

A Southern Methodist media specialist I know was raised in a family that stifled humor in women. "We weren't supposed to be funny and we were always cautioned against having a boisterous laugh. It wasn't until recently, when invited to speak to groups, that I learned I had a good sense of humor. The laughter was music to my ears. It's the favorite new quality I found out about myself."

My Italian, Irish, and Jewish friends often grew up in households where laughter was a staple. If humor comes out of pain and poverty, these groups had all three. Author Maurice Sendak said he grew up Jewish in Hell's Kitchen with Italian and Irish friends. He never knew the difference among them, and always thought that "the Italians were the happy Jews, and the Irish . . . were the depressed ones."

Some of the best humorists among my National Speakers Association colleagues are men and women from the South. Their regional humor and delivery is very different from my Chicago–New York ethnic style, and I enjoy their take on events and stories.

CAUTION: Just because someone tells a joke about "their group," don't think that it's acceptable for you to do the same. I may share an anecdote of Mumsy's recommendations for a forehead lift—and liposuction (yes, she has suggested that as well!)—but it would not be prudent for someone else to use my anecdote (it's my story to tell) or to suggest that Mumsy is really onto something.

SENSITIVE *SHTICK*

Be sensitive to your audience. Different people respond differently to different types of humor.

Sherwood Cummins of Recreate is my personal trainer. While I am working, lifting, huffing, and puffing, he shares his wonderful humor. However, he loves long, involved shaggy dog stories, and I don't. We talked about it and now he only shares those "jokes" with a one-two punch. And I'm a happier client. (The longer the setup, the better the punch line has to be.)

It's wonderful to hang out with people who are full of fun, stories, and laughter—but humor should never become a competition to see who has the better punch line or the quicker wit. Who's got it bigger, better, faster, funnier? A game that declares winners often has losers.

Humor calls for judgment, and the cost of the quip can be incalculable. Is this the right time and place for that particular joke? Even a thought-provoking exchange can be derailed by an ill-timed attempt at humor.

Shana attended a social dinner at a friend and colleague's home with others who shared varying degrees of social and business friendships. "I was telling a story that related to our discussion," she said. "Halfway through my tale, Ann felt compelled to interject a very funny one-liner. After the laughter subsided, I continued and the story started a discussion, which Ann again interrupted with a quip. This time I was ticked off, because the interruption was clearly ill-timed and ill-mannered. I turned to her and quietly said, 'Obviously you weren't listening.' We all went back to the discussion, and the evening opened into a group interchange."

Ann's humor was inappropriate to that situation. Rather than building group conversation, she was interrupting and refocusing the attention on herself. While she may have been very funny, the results were not. Shana and Ann are colleagues who could do business together and refer business to each other—and Shana has no intention of ever referring business to Ann again.

Keep in mind where you're going with humor before you start down the "funny" road.

AT&T TEST

How do we know if a story, comment, or joke is appropriate? Apply the AT&T rule as a litmus test. Is it:

- Appropriate?
- Timely?
- Tasteful?

Times have changed, and will continue to change. What was appropriate in 1968 or 1988 may not be so in 1998 or 2008.

A gentleman in a program I gave in Dallas said that he has a simple guideline. "Would I tell it to my mother?"

Another guideline: "Is this joke how I want my client, boss, or chairman of the board to remember me?"

MALE AND FEMALE FUNNY BONES TO PICK

Men and women have different styles of humor, according to research that has become common wisdom. Women tend to use self-deprecating humor and put themselves down, rather than putting down others. Phyllis Diller, Joan Rivers, Roseanne, and Fran Drescher are good examples. While there are limits to the uses of this humor—people are uncomfortable with statements that are *too* self-deprecating—it's not as dangerous as the ritual teasing and putting down of *one another* that characterizes men's humor. Don Rickles and Bobby Slayton come into mind.

Some men are perfectly comfortable dishing it out, and even taking it—but others are not as adept at this ritual. Proceed with great caution. The person you have teased, especially in front of the group, may not like it—but not let on until you take a job interview with him or her. You never know. Successful people make good judgment calls on this issue—and if they are off the mark, they apologize.

Both "male" and "female" tendencies in humor lend themselves to trouble and pitfalls. Skilled conversationalists can't afford to get stuck in either pattern.

CROSSING CLERICAL LINES: THE FRIAR'S ROAST

The clergy is another place to be careful with humor. The best ten-minute speech I ever gave was in honor of Father Larry Lorenzoni, a Salesian priest and well-known pundit who was on his way to work at the Vatican.

I had been prepped with the following: "To represent Father Larry's new friends, at his dinner, we want you to do a five- to ten-minute roast."

That made me nervous, so I clarified the instructions. "Let's see. You want me to get up in front of 250 of Father Larry's friends, parishioners and colleagues, other priests and bishops? In front of the Roman Catholic congregates and clergy, you want me to *roast* a priest! I don't think so! The gods would go crazy."

I proceeded with a loving, lively, lighthearted tribute— a toast, not a roast. It felt better to me—more appropriate and more ecumenical.

HUMOR = TRAGEDY + TIME

The ancient prophets had it right. How often have we heard, "You'll laugh about this tomorrow"?

We never believe it, but as we tell the story for the third or fourth time, we find ourselves adding inflections or pauses that lighten up the event. Our listeners laugh. And then we do, too.

According to the Talmud, a lesson learned with laughter is a lesson remembered. I wish I had known that as a teacher in Chicago!

Humor and lighthearted conversation helps us laugh and enjoy life. Laughing together creates camaraderie, can establish commonality, and definitely contributes to conversation. If you are a person of good humor, the room "works" you.

REMINDERS

- **Humor is tragedy plus time.**
- **A lighthearted attitude attracts others.**
- **Put-downs and off-color jokes and stories may be off-putting. Avoid humor at the expense of others.**
- **Listen for the funny stories in everyday life. Write them down, and practice them with the punch line at the end.**
- **Remember the AT&T test: Appropriate, Timely, Tasteful.**

CHAPTER 8

HOW TO SHINE IN A CROWD

It's the cocktail party following your company's annual meeting, an industry convention, a trade show, a fund-raiser, or your nephew's wedding. It's a huge room full of people, several hundred of them—most of whom you don't know.

You need to mix, mingle, meet people, and be sociable. But how? Where do you start?

This chapter is about how to shine in any crowd, and how to turn a room full of strangers from a daunting experience into an opportunity for business and social success—and have fun in the process.

WHO *ARE* THESE PEOPLE?

Easily 90 percent of the people we meet at these events work hard, have families and hobbies, and suffer and enjoy the same weather, economy, and computer glitches that we do. They have favorite sports teams, restaurants, music, and books. Whether their title is boss, board member, client, colleague, co-worker or friend, that's what people do. They live life.

Not only are most of us human beings pretty nice, but we have a lot in common with one another. Most of us were raised to be thoughtful and well-mannered, and we want to be good conversationalists.

So the first thing to remember as we step into that crowd is that people want to talk to us. They are just as eager as we are to make connections, to be relaxed, and to talk, share, and get to know others.

There may be a few people who have trouble expressing that part of themselves, and they may come across as too busy or important to talk to us, or bored, or simply aloof—but with most of us, this is just a mask to cover up the fear of being vulnerable.

There are a few others who "overwork" the room, "putting themselves out there" for fun or profit in ways that are embarrassing and seem insincere—but they, too, may just be covering up their nervousness.

Walking into this kind of crowd with confidence and comfort is a question of attitude—the attitude of liking other people, and wanting to get to know and connect with them.

Our tool for making those connections is conversation. Woody Allen was wrong when he said, "Eighty percent of life is just showing up." Showing up is *not* enough; it is only how we open the door. If we don't step into the room, we miss out on all the opportunities inside.

I once attended a banquet for more than a hundred people honoring Gwen Chan, my longtime friend and neighbor, as San Francisco's Schoolmaster of the Year. All eight of us at our table had in common our friendship with Gwen and an interest in education, yet the only person who introduced himself to me was the late-arriving basketball coach, whose team had just lost a game by three points. I was the outsider in the group, but how we treat outsiders speaks volumes about our social ability, manners, group graciousness, and conversational skills.

Whenever I feel hesitant about extending myself to a new person, especially in a group, I remember how I felt that night. Then I walk over and introduce myself.

A GREAT, NOT GRAND, ENTRANCE

Whether entering a cocktail party for hundreds, a conference hall, a ballroom, or a ball game, stop and take a deep breath. Survey the setting, so you get the lay of the land (and land mines). Where are the bars? The buffet? The groups? The people standing alone? Get a feel for how people are behaving. Walk in with your head held high, and head for the host, the greeter, or people you recognize (provided you don't stay with them throughout the event).

You still have butterflies in your stomach? To successfully "schmooze in a crowd," we need to prepare ourselves and practice the strategies that contribute to our comfort and conversational success. What is it that keeps us from being at ease with meeting and mingling? Let's look at some of the specific, identifiable roadblocks—and the remedies we can use to overcome them.

THE "STRANGERS IN THE NIGHT"—OR DAY— PITFALL

When we were growing up, our parents may have told us, "Don't talk to strangers."

Some of us are still unconsciously following that advice, even though it's not very useful as we manage or change our careers, grow our businesses, or enjoy our lives. If we avoid strangers at our professional association luncheon, a chamber of commerce mixer, or a client-sponsored soiree, we'll not only have a terrible time, we'll miss opportunities.

Remedy: Redefine "strangers." Think of them as "friends we haven't met yet." Or possibly "people with whom we share a commonality": a profession or trade, a business community, an interest in the Special Olympics, literacy, breast cancer, or volunteerism. That commonality gives us a basis for conversation.

Tip: Before you go anywhere, *think about what you have in common with the people attending the event.* This is permanently assigned homework, guaranteed to send you to the head of the class. Once you've established a common thread with them, topics for conversation become obvious. That leads to confidence, which attracts people.

THE "PROPER INTRODUCTION" PITFALL

Many of us were taught to speak only to people to whom we've been "properly introduced." And we wait for someone else to do the work of introducing us, preferably with the enthusiasm and energy that Ed McMahon conveyed for Johnny Carson.

THE BAD NEWS IS, IT AIN'T GONNA HAPPEN! We are on our own.

Remedy: Have a planned, practiced seven- to nine-second animated self-introduction.

Tips: Here are some tips for *introducing yourself:*

SELF-INTRODUCTION TIPS

1. Make your introduction seven to nine seconds in length. (The thirty-second or longer self-promotional pitch is *not* appropriate.)
2. Lean into the introduction. "Extending" yourself is a trait of great hosts. Just be mindful that everyone needs twelve to eighteen inches of personal space, and don't go inside that.
3. Accompany your introduction with a smile and firm web-to-web handshake. (Avoid the squeeze.)
4. Be creative. Add more than name, rank, and serial number. For business, give people the benefit of what you do.

Here's an example. Computer consultant and Web master Ken Braly says, "Hi, I'm Ken Braly. I erase the fear of computers for technophobes. Glad to meet you." Ken's face, stance, and tone *reinforce* that he is glad. (Remember, behavior that doesn't support our words subverts them.)

Ken's introduction gives enough information, and creates enough curiosity, that people can ask:

- "What does that mean?"
- "Who do you work with?"
- "How can you turn me from technophobe to techno-nerd?"

Or they can respond:

- "Wow! I could use your help." (my comment)
- "I have a friend who is scared of his computer and is losing business because of it."

To which Ken can answer:

- "Here's my card. Let's set a time to get together and talk."
- "What kind of business does your friend have?"

The more information we give in that seven to nine seconds, the more hooks we give the other person to pursue.

Deliver your introduction with energy, enthusiasm, facial expression, and appropriate animation—but remember: This book is not *Attila's Guerrilla Guide to Shark-Infested Negotiation*. It's about social intercourse, verbal communication, and the art of conversation to bolster your success in business and social situations. I leave the strategies for maneuvering, mangling, manipulating, and "overworking" the room to others.

THE "FEAR OF SMALL TALK" PITFALL: KEEPING OPEN THE DISNEY "CHANNELS OF COMMUNICATION"

We have seen that some people actually avoid "small talk" so they won't be perceived as shallow. That's a belief we have to give up if we're going to enjoy ourselves and flourish in groups.

Remedy: Remember that casual conversation is how we begin the communication process. Not many people are comfortable walking up to someone and starting a conversation about Bosnia, nuclear proliferation, famine in Africa, or the rape of the rain forest.

Tip: Start small and build. It's easier to start with a topic like the reason everyone is gathered together in the first place, the unusual weather, people's occupations, or even the lovely broccoli flowerettes on the buffet. Casual conversation is how we nurture and "grow" relationships—and those relationships can blossom in amazing and unexpected ways. *Small talk builds rapport, respect, and relationships.*

The 1995 Michael² (Ovitz and Eisner) match began as casual conversation, and these two buddies consummated the deal making ABC a new Disney Channel not in a boardroom or at a power lunch, but during a hike on a family vacation.

We can't expect that someone will "slip us a Mickey" Mouse deal at each event we attend, but I always apply the **RoAne Theory of Business and Marketing: You Never Know!**

Go to the event with a focus, but be open to serendipity—the stuff that happens while we are planning something else!

THE "WAITING FOR GODOT" PITFALL

Another childhood maxim: "Good things come to those who wait." Not when it comes to mingling! The RoAne version for the twenty-first century: *Good things come to those who initiate.*

Remedy: Remember that if we wait around for people to come over to us, all we get is gray hair, wrinkles, and varicose veins from standing around.

Tip: Review why you chose to attend the event, and don't leave home without accomplishing that purpose. It will give you the courage and enthusiasm to walk across the room, look someone in the eye, and introduce yourself.

> *"Because it is simple does not make it easy."*
> —*I'll Fly Away,* **PBS**

BACK TO BASICS: THE PLEASANTRIES

When in doubt, we can always fall back on a standard, appropriate greeting—followed by some pleasantries. "Pleasantries" is a word that suggests warmth and courtesy, which we can communicate with smiles, energy, and solid handshakes.

Here's how it works:

SO: "Hello, I'm Sally Osmun, supervisor of our West Coast sales offices. So nice to meet you."

LC: "Nice to meet you, too. I'm Larry Cohen with the branch office in Sioux City. Which of our West Coast offices is your base?"

SO: "Carmel."

LC: "Lucky you! I was only there three days and fell in love with the area. I have always wanted to play eighteen holes at Pebble Beach."

SO: "I don't play golf, but my golfing friends are convinced it is one of the best. I've gone to the PGA tournament, as our company sponsors a hospitality suite." (Back to business.)

LC: "Does the Pebble Beach sponsorship benefit our company? Impact sales?"

We don't have to know everything, or even a lot, about a subject in order to make conversation about it. We just need to be well-read or well-versed enough to ask good questions or rely on our friends' experience, as Sally did with Pebble Beach.

THE MAGIC FORMULA: ACT LIKE A HOST

Skills for Success author Dr. Adele Scheele suggests that successful socializers don't wait around behaving like guests. Instead, they should take their innate gracious attitude to every event and act like they are the *host*.

Hosts are interested in other people's comfort, and go out of their way to mix, mingle, and connect people. They greet others, make them feel welcome, introduce them to others, share stories, ask questions, and *listen to the responses*. Hosts cheerfully and politely excuse themselves once the new kid is settled into a conversation.

The magical part is that people tell me, "I never thought I could or should take charge like that, but when I consider it 'my job' to meet people, put them at ease, keep the conversation flowing, and introduce them to one another, *I'm actually more relaxed myself.*"

There are two parts to mingling—being *interesting,* and being *interested.* "Acting like the host" reminds us to do both. If we are interested in others, we create a memorable impression. That means people are left with more than our business card when the event is over.

Tip: If you really *are* the host, or host organization, be sure to act like it! Be welcoming, warm, and "word-er-ful."

THE GREETING COMMITTEE

Volunteering for the greeting committee is a great way to sharpen our hosting skills. It then becomes our *job* to meet, greet, or introduce other guests.

We have to push through whatever discomfort we feel, and we get a chance to practice self-introductions and chatting. Both become easier and more natural with time.

As greeters, we also get to meet and speak with the most people. Making people feel welcome feels good. it draws people to us, and makes us more confident.

Greeters learn that the "80-20 Rule"—80 percent of people are nice and welcome our conversation, 20 percent do not—isn't quite true. It's more like 90-10 percent. The rewards of hosting and greeting are well worth the risk.

PREPARATION POLICY: THE HIGH FIVE

It's easier to shine in a crowd when we feel confident, and we feel confident when we are prepared. Here are some areas to prepare:

1. *ATTITUDE.* Savvy socializers say they "look forward" to events. They like people and "find them interesting."
2. *FOCUS.* Have a purpose for attending, whether it is to gain visibility, make contacts, or create goodwill or good public relations. (*Caveat:* We must be guided by our goals, not blinded by them!)
3. *CARDS.* Have enough, have them accessible, and have them readable. Use them to follow up conversation, not replace it.
4. *CONVERSATION.* Come to the event with five open-ended questions and five stories or topics you have practiced.
5. *A SMILE.* Accompany your smile with eye contact, which is the key indication that we are open and "in the moment" with our conversation partners.

Being approachable means having a pleasant countenance, visual connection, and a welcoming stance. No one ever says, "Oh look, there's a glowering, glaring sourpuss I must meet!"

To be approachable, we must also be appropriate. Some authors and experts advise us to be outrageous, to dress outrageously and say outrageous things, in order to be memorable. But "being memorable" can backfire, if it's for a comment or behavior that made people uncomfortable. Be sensible, and remember to use good judgment.

THE NOSH AND NIBBLE NETWORK HOUR™

When there is food at an event, we tend to eat it without thinking. Eating and mingling require balance, literally and figuratively, and we have to keep our wits about us.

It is always inappropriate to converse with a mouth full of food, or to pile a plate so full that others notice. It is also difficult to juggle food, beverage, and business cards. The best way to win the "balance act" is to eat first and wash our hands (or use a towelette). If we wear lipstick, now's the time to reapply.

Then circulate.

> *"Never eat more than you can lift."*
>
> —MISS PIGGY

LIQUID ASSETS?

Let me put the drink debate to rest. At a business or quasi-business social event, we want to be sure our behavior is an asset. When it comes to liquid refreshments, be conservative.

What can nondrinkers do in companies that have a hard-charging and hard-drinking culture? Some just stick to club soda and continue to converse. Others hold a drink, but don't drink it. Some ConverSensations and corporate experts I interviewed said that being a nondrinker was *not* a problem. Others said that although they themselves were comfortable with nondrinkers, some of their drinking colleagues were not.

At events with a network of potential clients, moderation is the mantra.

"The only proper intoxication is conversation."
—OSCAR WILDE

NAME TAG TIPS

Always, always wear your name tag on the right-hand side. That puts it in the other person's line of sight as you both extend your right arm for a handshake. If the name tag is one you fill out yourself, use a thick marker so it can be seen. Write something to pique people's curiosity—perhaps something that suggests a benefit to them.

Examples:

- A massage therapist wrote: "PAINKILLER." That was provocative and gave others a hook for questions.
- A doctor with a good sense of humor wrote: "MEDICINE MAN."

Name tags are conversation starters. If you are hosting a traditional conference where name tags are preprinted from a computer database, make sure the program prints the names IN LARGE TYPE. If company, title, and city are on the name tag, people can use the information to start a conversation.

"Oh, I see you're from Indianapolis. Is that as nice a city as I hear?"

Rhonda Abrams, syndicated small-business columnist and consultant, says that at both business and social events she finds "Where are you from originally?" to be a good opener. In San Francisco, where natives are not abundant, this starts the volley. And if someone is actually from San Francisco, it's an even better conversation starter.

THE NAME GAME: I FORGOT!

People don't remember names. According to Dr. Anneliese Batius, a psychiatrist at Harvard Medical School, "Forgetting is part of the normal memory system." Memory lapses are natural.

What should we do if we forget a name?

Tips:

1. *Tell the Truth.* Don't waste your time trying to remember how you were supposed to remember this person's name, something about "putting a cat in a vat on a hat on someone's head." Instead, simply say, *"It's been one of those days. I remember you, but please tell me your name."* Say it lightly and slightly apologetically. People understand. It's happened to them!

2. *Stick your hand out and say your name.* People respond in kind 90 percent of the time. Believe me, if you forgot their name, they've probably forgotten yours. By saying your name, you alleviate their discomfort and give them a chance to reveal their name. That way, nobody struggles with the name game embarrassment.

There's no point to the cruel game of putting someone on the spot about your name. This is not how to start an engaging conversation. ConverSensations do not do this. Successful communicators build bridges, they don't burn them.

THE NAME GAME

Wrong greeting: "Hey, Joan, it's great to see you after all these years."
Correct Greeting: "Hello. I'm Sherman Oaks. Nice to see you again."
Response: "Joan D'Arc from the Paris office. Good to see you, too."
Absolute Worst Greeting: "Hey, Joan, do you remember me?"

Make an effort to remember people's names. Read their name tag or repeat the name if you're introduced. Think about the person and look at them as you say the name. Focus on that person, not on your next conversational tidbit. Do what you can to remember, but be forgiving if you forget.

Mingling mavens are civil people. We let others save

face and cut people slack. At a chamber mixer, I was introduced to a woman and said, "Nice to meet you."

Her response, with ice in her voice, was, "We already met." Oops! Gulp!

A better, more gracious response would have been, "Nice to see you again. I'm Carmen Sandiego."

CONVERSATION STARTERS

It's easier to approach one person, instead of two or more. But what if that person is a bit shy, new, or just uncomfortable? Here are some ice-melters:

"Hi, I'm Oscar Meyer.
1. "Are you a member?
2. "How often have you attended this trade show?
3. "Your tie is great. Is it a Jerry Garcia? (Even if it isn't, you may have found a fan, maybe even a Dead head. And that's another trip!)
4. "Have you been to the museum (venue) before?
5. "This hotel looks fabulous since the remodel."

Say something. Anything. Do *not* wait for the brilliant opening line. There is no such thing. "Hi!" or "Hello!" is always a good opener that encourages a person to respond in kind.

Remember: It's called a "line" for a reason. And people don't "cotton to" lines—hearing them or waiting in them.

THE "WHO'S WHO"

How do we approach people in positions of power? With manners, respect, and appropriate etiquette. Use titles

(Dr., Senator, Mayor, Reverend, Duke, Rabbi, Your Honor, Lieutenant, General, Detective, Mr. or Ms.), and only move to a first name when invited to do so. Don't presume familiarity. Is this old-fashioned? Perhaps, but what's the risk? That someone will accuse us of having good, old-fashioned manners? We should live so long! The alternative is to risk being memorable for mangled manners.

CONVERSATION STARTERS

Common experience is always a good conversation starter. Try:

- The organization or cause
- The venue
- The view
- The food (taste or lack thereof); beware of *kvetching*
- "Please pass the . . ." "Would you like the . . . (rolls, salad dressing, sugar, Equal or not equal)?"
- Offering a comment like "I had a great lunch last week at the Convention and Visitors Bureau."
- Respond with a question like "Oh? Where was it held?"

BREAKING AND ENTERING

How do we join in when people are already gathered in groups, having conversations and a good time?

First, minimize this problem by showing up no more than fifteen minutes after the appointed time. Research on shy people indicates that they do this to avoid having to enter a room full of people. If you are one of the "early birds," people are more likely to come over to you—especially if you smile and make eye contact.

If you have just walked into a "gathering in progress," first introduce yourself to the host or greeter. Then scan the room and look for the most animated group of three to five people. (It's tougher to go over to two people, since they could be engaged in an intimate or otherwise important conversation. With two people we might be interrupting; with three or more we are joining.)

To get into a group, stand on the periphery with open, agreeable body language and sounds ("hm, mmm"), nodding and smiling. When someone invites you by words, eye contact, or facial expression to step into the group, you can introduce yourself and say something pleasant. Don't be afraid you'll have nothing to contribute. It is highly unlikely that they will be discussing quantum physics or other subjects about which you may know nothing.

Warning: This is not the time for a thirty-second self-promotional pitch! We are an invited guest in this conversation, not the star. Believe it or not, there are some people who have asked me just how to get into groups and change "small talk" conversations to business. And it is always about *their* business, *their* agenda. My answer is always, "Very carefully, or not at all."

Another strategy for breaking and entering a group is to ask a question or make a comment that relates to the discussion. But be careful. Questions or comments about oranges in a conversation about apples are jarring. Here are some good questions:

- "What did you think of . . . ?"
- "Have you heard . . . ?"
- "What is your take on . . . ?"
- "Yes, but . . ." or better, "Yes, and . . ."
- "As a thought on . . ."
- "Have you considered the impact on seniors? (and without hesitation) My great-aunt lives in senior housing and she and her friends are very concerned about the managed-care package."

You can also break and enter with a compliment, or by agreeing with the speaker. Robert Mayer, author of *Power Plays,* is a proponent of the "alignment tactic": "Agree with the speaker and link it to your viewpoint. The agreement takes the sting out of the interruption."

GROUP TALK: WHY WE LOVE IT

Human beings love face-to-face encounters. The "salon movement" has proliferated because people *want* to come together with other dynamic, interested, and interesting people to talk in groups about issues and ideas that have substance. These salons include support groups, special interest groups, and book clubs. Dr. Victor Harnack of the University of Illinois says that if salons are the front porch for those who want to see their conversation partners, then the Internet is our electronic front porch of today.

Although we all have our own preferences for what a "good" conversation is, great group talk is a conversation that is interesting, has energy, is inclusive, and builds on the comments and contributions of the people involved. The pleasantries exchanged are pleasant. It can also be thought-provoking, informative, and fun.

To keep the conversation moving along these lines, we have to exercise good judgment. Will our comments *add* to the conversation and build on what is being said? Or will they interrupt and shift the attention to us? Is the risk of doing so—and possibly annoying the person who is talking—worth it? If we believe we can add energy and improve the quality of the group conversation, the answer may be yes.

In these judgment calls, consider two things:

1. *The Group.* Who is in it? Bosses, competitors, co-workers, relatives? What is each person's position?
2. *Your Comment* (remark, response, retort). Could it have a boomerang effect in this group? Will it lend itself to clear boundary setting? Could it be construed as confrontational? Could it create discomfort? Will it change the dynamics? Will it address the issue or remedy the situation? Will it offend one person? (If you offend one, it could cost you the group.)

"Character is tested through three things: business, wine, and conversation."
—ABUT DE RABBI NATHAN 31

GROUP SPEAK:
BUILDING A GROUP CONVERSATION

Here's an example of how group conversations can begin and build. The setting is a professional event in a hotel in Sweltering City, Anywhere, U.S.A. . . .

PERSON 1: "The air-conditioning in our office building broke down so the boss gave us the afternoon off to go home early to 'sweat it out,' literally."

PERSON 2: "So, how many people actually left?"

P1: "I was surprised at how many did leave, and that those who left were at all levels in the company."

PERSON 3: "Did the building get hot immediately after the breakdown?"

P1: "No, actually it remained cool, because of the insulation, for another hour and a half. Then we left, including the CEO. It became difficult to breathe!"

P3: "I guess the air from the outside, with no wind, wouldn't have been much help."

P1: "That's a problem. Our office building is also from that architectural no-window era, my least favorite."

(As Person 4 joins in.)

Person 4: "Give me windows. I much prefer fresh air to heat or air-conditioning, on most days."

P2: "Me, too. I am a fresh air fanatic. Whenever I'm on the road, I ask for a hotel room with a window that can be opened—of course, promising not to jump."

P3: "That's one of the reasons those with windows have such a small 'window of opportunity' for air."

P2: "If someone wants to jump, they'll find a way. All I want is fresh air."

P3: "Then you may want to stay out of Los Angeles this month. I was just there for a meeting downtown, with skies of brown. Couldn't wait to get back home, although the meeting with Castle Rock went well."

P1: "Are you getting into movies?"

P3: "No, we're exploring a joint venture . . ."

This four-person conversation builds, shifts, varies in tone, gives information, and discusses issues. *The key is that each participant has listened and adds to the flow*. Nobody tries to redirect it or focus it on themselves.

It contains the three elements of conversation we discussed in Chapter 4, the OAR elements:

THE THREE ELEMENTS OF GREAT CONVERSATION

- Offer an observation.
- Ask a question.
- Reveal your thoughts, ideas, or opinions.

YENTA, THE MATCHMAKER

The best of minglers are the conversationalists who bring others into the group with enough information, enthusiasm, and respect to make the group want to include the "new kid on the block." Even when she has just met the new person, "Yenta" remembers most of what was said and adds that into the mix.

LUKEWARM INTRODUCTION: *"Jane, meet Joe."*

YENTA'S INTRODUCTION: *"Jane is our accountant and a marathon runner. Joe is our union representative. He has a fascinating hobby; he wind-surfs all over the world."*

Introductions should create a warm reception and "make a match." Terri Lonier, author of *Working Solo,* calls them "Power Partner" introductions that promote conversation.

SHINING THE LIGHT IN A CROWD

Those who shine in the crowd have another universal trait: They shine the light on others in the crowd.

Patricia Fripp is one of the best at doing this. Although she is a well-known national public speaker, and often recognized, she always shines the light on others. She starts off by sharing an enthusiastic comment or two about the new person, and then easing them into the group conversation. Patricia acts like a host. She includes people with eye contact, words, body language, and her welcoming presence.

When you extend yourself to someone and invite them into your group conversation, you become not only well-mannered, but also memorable. People do remember and refer business to someone who has included them, rather than excluded them.

ROUND TABLE TALK

There you are at the chamber of commerce, conference board, or professional association luncheon or dinner, seated at a round table with several other attendees. No more moving around for a while. You're stuck where you are, and have only limited choices of people with whom to make conversation. Sometimes it's a blessing to be "stuck" with someone; sometimes it's not. In either case, make the most of it. Engage the people on either side with pleasantries and small talk.

Here are some ways to break, or at least melt, the ice:

ICE-MELTERS

- "Are you a member?"
- "This is my first time at this (restaurant, hotel, venue)."
- "I've wanted to come back to the St. Francis Yacht Club since it was renovated."
- "What prompted you to attend today's event?" (When I am the speaker, I love to hear I am the reason!)
- "Would you mind passing the rolls? They look so good, I can't resist. It could be worse . . . a jelly doughnut!"

HOT TALK TIP: In *Power Schmoozing,* my friend Terri Mandell suggests that saying more about yourself, an extra phrase or two, helps others build and contribute to the conversation.

What about the other people, the ones *across* the table, whom you would like to meet? Carl LaMell, Executive Director of Clearbrook Center, a Chicago-based nonprofit agency, recommends "taking the bull by the horns" and giving everyone a chance by inviting them to self-introduce.

"I often will say, 'I'd love to meet you all. Why don't we go around the table and introduce ourselves?' People are grateful because they want to be included and have the opportunity to introduce themselves." You may prefer waiting to do this until people are eating, the room is quieter, and you don't have to scream over the din.

Again, be the host. The person across the table may be the one with whom you end up doing business, playing tennis, or trading referrals.

> **"These things are good in small quantities and bad in large: yeast, salt, and hesitation."**
> —THE TALMUD

DEALING WITH THE ROTTEN APPLE

I've always believed I could handle tough audiences as a professional speaker, and tough groups as a mingler, because I used to teach sixth grade!

Occasionally we run across someone who throws a monkey wrench into everything that happens in the group. The hogger of attention, the inappropriate joke-ster, the sexist good old boy, the tippler, the chronic inter-rupter, the too-hard back slapper, and a host of others can make almost any group unpleasant.

When someone has the bad judgment to step on your toes, or the group's toes, here are some countermeasures that are particularly useful for people who interrupt you at inappropriate times:

- Laugh with the group and continue.
- Don't laugh, and continue.
- Say nothing, and don't continue. Maybe the message is, "It's time to share the floor."
- Say lightly, "Well, I guess that ends my story."
- If you want to say something to a two-time transgres-sor, pull them aside and express your action in "I" mes-sages. Or, maybe just shoot a look.

Warning: Even though an adult "misbehaves," it may not be the time, place, or group in which to handle the situation, especially if business is involved.

Also remember that the group may be fascinated by something that we find absolutely boring. As a Boston-based CPA, Lana Teplick attends many all-day seminars to keep up with the changes in her industry. "I can't spend four hours in an accounting seminar, then spend the lunch hour discussing the IRS! I prefer to talk to my colleagues as people, about kids, about current events, about the Celtics. But I've come to realize that sometimes the other accountants really want to spend lunchtime discussing the IRS. I have to figure out when that is and adjust—or just stop and be quiet, not taking the group off its desired course of conversation.

If a group wants to discuss a subject in which we are not interested, we can either be polite, be quiet, or be gone.

BE GRACIOUS, BE BRIEF, BE GONE

When we meet the important host, guest, or honoree, we should be pleasant but not hog his or her time with our agenda—especially if there is a line of people who also want to meet Mr./Ms. Important. Our agenda is not the priority at that moment. If we do talk to the important person about our concerns, we want it to be when that agenda *can* be the priority.

We may say that there is something we want to discuss, and ask what would be the best way to contact him or her. That gives Mr./Ms. Important the option of saying, "Let's take a minute now," or "Call my office and ask for Bob."

Do as they ask, and follow up with a note saying, "Thank you for your time and direction."

PARTING IS SUCH SWEET SORROW

Extricating and exiting from a conversation (and every aspect of life) can be excruciating. If we observe body language and nonverbal signals—fidgeting, glancing around the room, shifting feet, wandering attention—we can tell when our partner is ready to exit. We are memorable if we notice the signals and facilitate the ending.

Here are three ways to do so:

1. *Friendly recap* of what you discussed that emphasizes your connection: "It's been fun talking to a kindred spirit who enjoys watching *The Nanny* as much as I do. I'll let you know if I hear that Fran Drescher has a local book signing."

2. *Get me outta here.* If the exchange was not particularly fun, lively, or interesting, we can just excuse ourselves and say with an upbeat tone, "I hope you enjoy the rest of the event (party, conference, ballet, picnic, etc.)."

3. *The total truth.* This, I'm afraid, works only in special circumstances. At a national sorority's regional Panhellenic luncheon where I spoke, one of the U.C. Berkeley alums was ninety-six and still attended all the events. One of her "younger" sorority sisters told me Jane's exiting remark was always, *"If you'll excuse me, I now must go and mingle."* At ninety-six, you get to say whatever you want! It might work for you, too, if said with spirit and a tone that's both light and polite.

Instead of leaning into the exit, we move slightly back. The conversation was summarized or an exchange acknowledged. The next step is to move about one quarter of the room away—over to someone else or another group.

Remember: If the person wasn't particularly warm or receptive, it may have had nothing to do with you. He or she may have just learned that one of his children did poorly on the SATs, that her mother may have fallen and broken a hip, or that the company may be downsizing. Or he or she might just be coming down with the flu. You never know. Regardless of how your exchange went, be polite.

Another way to exit is the "Come on Along" approach used by Dr. Irving Siegel, founding fellow of the American College of Obstetricians and Gynecologists. At a conference, he acts like a host and will often say to a young doctor, *"Dr. Baumann, I see Dr. Glasser. Why don't you join me and I'll introduce you?"*

Rather than leave the person, Dr. Siegel introduces him to colleagues and helps him increase his comfort, contacts, and collegial circle. That is memorable—and each of us can do it!

MEDICAL MINGLING REMINDERS

Remember that some of us need for you to speak more loudly and more clearly. And some of us may have early arthritis or carpal tunnel syndrome, so don't squeeze our hands too hard.

If you have a specific problem, just say, *"I'd love to shake your hand, but I just sprained my thumb."* That gives the person information and an explanation. Otherwise, you might be perceived as rude and standoffish. This is another case in which the truth can start a conversation. You've disclosed something about yourself, and given information that could prompt questions or comments. And that's what we want to do—share that which will spark interest, questions, and comments.

SPOUSAL SUPPORT: YOURS AND THEIRS

Remember, our associates' spouses have a great deal of influence, so we must include and be gracious to them. Not doing so can create a lasting poor impression.

Many accompanying spouses are now male (10 percent of the spouses at the American College of Surgeons convention are men), but the majority are still women who are smart, intelligent, and involved either in their own careers or in the community. We all share experiences of the weather, community issues (traffic, parking, road repairs, school bonds and programs, literacy and library issues), political events, sports, arts, and cultural events that are easy to discuss with spouses.

How we talk to our *own* spouses in public is also important. Showing them respect and civility raises both them and us in people's eyes—and I have heard comments about people who made others uncomfortable by being less than gracious to their own spouses.

CORRECTION FLUID, FLUID CORRECTIONS

It's as much how we say things as what we say. At certain times, we may need to correct people who have made inaccurate or misleading comments—but there is a right time, place, and manner for these corrections, and it's often not in front of others.

Make it easy for people to save face and self-correct. "I was under the impression that it was a 2 percent increase," is better than "Where did you hear *that* figure? It hasn't been 4 percent in *twenty years!*"

Let good judgment and common sense prevail, and call off the detail guards. If it doesn't really matter, let it go. I was at a holiday dinner recently where our gracious host was recalling the longevity of this particular historic and religious observance. A guest piped up and corrected him. I knew my host's historic recollection was off fifty years but chose to say nothing. When I saw the look on his face after being corrected, and felt the heaviness in the air, I was delighted when another guest lightened the moment by saying, "After five thousand years, it's easy to lose count!"

THE VELVET GLOVE

As shocking as it may seem, we do not attend conferences, meetings, picnics, or fund-raisers just so we can sell our wares!

The tacit agreement at business functions is that it is about business—but no one signed on strictly to hear our spiel. We earn the right to "our say" by being part of the group dynamic, and by building conversation, rapport, and relationships.

If the conversation lags, we may pick it up by saying, "I joined you late, so I didn't catch your names, ranks, serial numbers. By the way, I'm Shelly Berger." It's a light way of asking for jobs, titles, and other important information.

People often talk about the event or venue, because that is what the commonality is, and the corporate golf tournament is famous for being a "soft sell" venue—so much so that both men and women are learning the game who really have minimal interest in chasing a little white ball around grassy hills for five hours on a Saturday afternoon.

The first conversations may be about the game itself, the course, other courses, the pros, golf stories and jokes, but somewhere out on the seventh or fourteenth hole, business is discussed. Even when the pro fixes up your foursome, by the fifth tee someone will ask, "What do you do?"

"Oh, I sell software."

"Really?" and so on.

I am not a golfer, but my sources say that business on the course is best kept very low-key—like the game itself. The good things about the conversation among the foursome are: 1) a captive audience and 2) a solid block of time.

The same process of conversation applies to tennis, hiking, biking, riding, backpacking, theater, musical performance in the intermissions, and so on.

OVER MY HEAD

There are times we feel that we don't know enough about a topic to contribute our thoughts in a group discussion. Remember "The Beauty of Not Knowing":

THE BEAUTY OF NOT KNOWING IS THAT:

1. All talkers need a listener and that is a memorable contribution. We participate with eyes, facial expressions, smiles, and nods of agreement.
2. This is a chance to learn something new. Interjecting "Wow!" or "Really?" is participating—as long as our enthusiasm is sincere. I often listen to "technonerds" discuss computers and Web sites in sheer amazement, and I convey my awe at their knowledge.
3. Just because someone else knows more than we do about a certain topic doesn't mean that we are lacking. As much as those lovable nerds know about electronic networking and motherboards, I know about personal networking and blackboards (we ex-teachers know how to chalk up a room).

Remember: We each have specific areas of knowledge—by vocation or avocation. Here is a quiz to identify your areas of expertise:

1. What do you do for money?
2. What do you do in your free time?
3. In what areas do people ask your advice?

MY FAVORITE THINGS TO DO		
FOR MONEY	FOR FREE	FOR ADVICE

We may not always get to share our knowledge and expertise, but it is important for our conversation confidence to *know what we know,* so that we can chime in when the opportunity presents itself.

It's a way to strengthen our self-esteem. When we have that, according to Dr. Nathaniel Branden, author of *The Six Pillars of Self-Esteem,* we are more likely to contribute our views to a conversation.

The bottom line is that we all have much to contribute to conversations, both verbally and nonverbally.

BEING PROVOCATIVE CAN PROVOKE

There are people who take great pride in being provocative. Several people I surveyed reported this as a technique that they used, or had seen used, successfully. One wrote about the woman she knew who always asked great questions at group functions, questions like, "If there were a fire, what would you save: your cat or your favorite painting?"

In some groups, that may work well—but proceed with caution. People don't like to be set up, and some topics could turn into debates. Another person shared the story of a cousin who "fancies herself a genius and a brilliant conversationalist. At a party hosted for my colleagues, we were all sitting around enjoying a relaxed conversation. The self-described brilliant conversationalist felt compelled to change the tone and tenor of the conversation by loudly posing a provocative political question. She does this a lot, and has no clue that she is clueless about group conversation dynamics."

To this woman, stirring up the brew was a positive thing to do, and being outspoken was a wonderful trait. Just beware of when, where, how, and why you do this. Being provocative can be provoking, and create negative memories that linger on.

Observing, understanding, honoring, and contributing . . . these are the keys to group conversational dynamics. A little charm, a dose of *chutzpah,* and you, too, will be a mingling maven—no matter how large the group.

REMINDERS

- The ability to work a room is the art of communication, which is made up of conversation, gestures, facial expressions, stance, and presence.
- Ninety percent of the people in any group are nice, raised to be polite, and have more in common than not.
- Just showing up is *not* enough.
- The person who shines in a crowd does three things:
  1. Focuses on the other person(s) with whom they are speaking, and engages each member with eye contact (up to eight seconds, after which it becomes a glare).
  2. Introduces others with enthusiasm.
  3. Has three to five planned pieces of conversation.
- Prepare for each event: Check your attitude, practice a seven- to nine-second self-introduction keyed to the event, and let your charm and *chutzpah* fly.
- Civility and good manners are telling.
- Introduce yourself to those who may look familiar by saying your name.
- Exercise good judgment. Observe and listen to group conversations before you contribute. Avoid derailing conversation by ill-timed funny lines.
- Build on comments from others in the group.
- Be inclusive. Act like the host.

CHAPTER 9

WORKING THE VIRTUAL CHAT ROOM: ON-LINE, NOT OUT-OF-LINE

Imagine the *chutzpah* it takes for me to write about cyberchat. I mean *write*, as sitting in Spinelli's coffeehouse with No. 2 pencils and a battery-operated sharpener in my *schlep* bag.

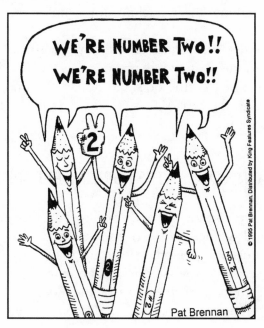

139

Yet being on-line just gives us another room to work—the room of the 1990s, a virtual chat room without walls that can include strangers who become our best friends or best contacts.

The number of people who converse on-line hit 30 million this year, and is growing exponentially. On-line communication is the telephone tree, the grapevine, the beauty shop, and barber shop of the 1990s—the popular way to banter, to schmooze, to engage in the exchange known as social intercourse, and to do formal and informal business.

It's also the Loehmann's of the message delivery world, a real bargain, especially compared to the cost of calls, mail, UPS, or even faxes.

There are a million stories in the naked city . . . about the wonders of e-mail. But e-mail has its own written and unwritten rules, and punishments for breaking them. We need to know the codes of behavior for bantering on-line, just as we follow the guidelines for mingling in real time and space.

Disclaimer: The controversy about cyber-smut and virtual sex rooms is beyond my purview. This chapter is about the how to's, the do's and don'ts, the endless possibilities, and the best M.O.'s (modems operandi) of conversing on-line.

LIKE IT OR NOT ... A HISTORICAL PERSPECTIVE

Whether we like it or not, we live in the electronic world—and we need to learn to live there *well*.

Computers and personal electronic mail are just the latest in a series of revolutions. Technology has impacted communication since the days of the Rosetta stone. We have Mr. Gutenberg's press, Mr. Marconi's telegraph, Mr.

Alexander Graham Bell's telephone, then television. And now this . . . a computer- and modem-based world known as the information superhighway.

Abandoned vehicles along the information superhighway.

While some people wax rhapsodic about cyberspace, others are skeptical. Dr. Philip Zimbardo, author of *Shyness: What It Is, What to Do About It,* has discovered that we are becoming less socially adept *and* increasingly shy because we are spending more time with our computers. We can do all our banking, for instance, without ever experiencing a word or smile from a friendly, flesh-and-blood teller. Some believe that's Progress at a Price.

"Computer companionship" may keep some kids from developing their reading, writing, or thinking skills—or knowing the joy of curling up with a good book. And there are those who warn that our conversation skills may be diminishing with computer usage. We heard similar warnings in the past about too much television, excessive interest in sports, and even inordinate amounts of book reading—and some experts believe that chat rooms actually increase our confidence and conversational competence. Moderation is probably the key, but go tell that to the fourteen-year-old who has just discovered a *Star Trek* forum or a cyber-soccer group!

We need to be *both* technically and socially adept to manage in the new millennium, and to succeed professionally and personally both in real space and in cyberspace.

MINGLING BY MODEM

I resisted the electronic on-line world even after a computer came to live with me. Then a cyber-savvy colleague, Bob Treadway, challenged me, "RoAne, how can you be the networking and mingling maven and *not* be part of the networked world?" He got my attention and I joined the twenty-first century—on-line.

There are several methods of "conversing" on-line: e-mail, chat rooms, forums, and World Wide Web postings. According to columnist Walter Mossberg of the *Wall Street Journal* (April 20, 1995), e-mail is the "most compelling, addictive and practical activity available on-line. It's also the simplest and least sexy."

E-mail is a way to converse, to touch base, and to nurture the relationships within our network of colleagues, cronies, clients and friends. Whether we run a business, manage a career, or are active in community organizations, it is a good idea to be available to converse on-line.

Mossberg points out both the personal and professional benefits of being on-line. He and his brother planned their parents' fiftieth wedding anniversary party on-line. A woman found her long-lost brother. Cures for syndromes and diseases have been shared. A couple found a baby to adopt, and many people have found jobs. My friend Sharon Arkin claims that she has never had so much communication with her far-flung adult children until they all got on-line. "Modem the Matchmaker" has even brought couples together.

E-mail also "flattens" organizations. We have access to the CEO without inching through the layers of hierarchy, simply by typing a message and hitting "Send"—but when we do e-mail the CEO, it had better be well-written, brief, and purposeful.

Another advantage of mingling by modem is that our race, religion, weight, and height do not matter. Our abilities are what's important; the information highway is an open venue.

Kate Macintosh was working at Intel after her first year as an MBA student at the University of Chicago. She was on a school program committee and wanted to invite Andy Grove, Intel's CEO, to speak—so she e-mailed him and extended the invitation. Because of her last name, she wrote a lighthearted comment about being a

Macintosh (no relation) at Intel. People could not believe she had the *chutzpah* to do it. But Kate said, "I had a good reason to communicate with Mr. Grove." Was she pleased with the response? "Even though he declined my invitation, his response was gracious, thoughtful and charming. I printed and saved it."

Electronic conversation can help begin or sustain a client, colleague, or personal relationship—but ultimately, our conversation has to be multidimensional. So pick up the phone to add the depth, width, or height that comes from communicating orally and aurally. Make a date, when geographically feasible, to get together for "the beverage break" so you can actually see one another and hear the laughter.

TECHNO-TRENDSETTERS

Dan Burrus, author of Technotrends, warns that to stay current and poised for the future, business must embrace technology. But, Burrus says, "technology does not run companies . . . relationships do. And technology can enhance relationships." That's what cyber-chat is all about—forging relationships.

Joan Eisenstodt is a highly regarded international meeting planner whom I met at a conference several years ago. We began to e-mail so we could set a "coffee break" time, and I have spoken at a convention based on her recommendation. Our friendship has deepened through e-mail, and so has our professional regard and support.

Electronic communication has its own upside-downside. While we can convey our information, thanks, regards, and regrets at our own convenience without having to invest time conversing with anyone, the downside is that we can do just that. We save time, but we can lose some of the richness of conversation if we're not careful.

E-MAIL-STROM

Conversing on-line is essential and fun, but it can be addictive. Kimberly S. Young, Ph.D., an on-line addiction researcher, has developed a simple quiz to identify the addict (*Marin Independent Journal,* May 27, 1995):

SIGNS YOU MAY BE HOOKED
A QUICK QUIZ

- Do you compulsively check your e-mail (ten to twenty times a day)?
- Do you lose track of time when you are on-line?
- Are you experiencing a problem in personal relations that can be blamed on the time you spend on-line?
- Have you gained weight or suffered eye, neck, or back strain from hours on-line?

If you answered yes to any of these questions, you may want to modify your moments with your modem. Go out to a movie, take a walk in the park, or go bowling—or, here's a thought—*read a book!* Off-line!

NETIQUETTE: A WORD TO THE "WIRED"

Cyber-etiquette, or "netiquette," was created to provide a structure of civility in what had been a rather unstructured form: the Internet. The Internet used to be the domain of the military and universities, but it has expanded to include eleven-year-olds, businesspeople, the medical and scientific community—and thee and me.

There is a lot of information available to help us converse and behave properly on-line—and it's important to know and respect the superhighway's rules of the road if we want to connect with and expand our network. If we don't, we could crash, burn, or even go up in flames! ("Flamed": multiple responses in the course of conversation, or an inappropriate use of the Internet.)

Dame Raquel writes in *Wired* (April 1995, p.162), "It is okay to ask if someone is male or female if they are using a 'handle.'" But we ought to be careful about gender. The person with whom we may presume an unwarranted familiarity may be a potential contact, client, or employer—and we could be *flamed*. The same commonsense rule applies to our visits to forums or chat rooms.

Ron Buono, a tax accountant, was setting up his wife's account at America Online so she could use it in her research as a teacher. Forgetting that the screen name he was using was his wife's, he entered a mountain bike chat room where he answered a technical question about gear ratios.

The first message he got back was, "What do you look like?" (This is a FAQ . . . frequently asked question.)

"I really had the feeling this was sexual harassment and I wanted to send an angry reply. Since I was acting under my wife's name, though, I decided to respond in a more rational manner. So I told the truth. My reply, 'I'm five feet eleven inches, weigh 195 pounds, and I have small hairs growing out of my ears!'

"'Good-bye,' flashed on my screen."

E-MAIL DO'S

Certain guidelines apply to polite and productive conversation in the electronic world, just as they do to the non-virtual world.

Here are the basics:

- Write brief e-mail messages.
- Forward messages only if permission has been granted by the originator (Dame Raquel, Network Diva, *Wired,* March 1995, p. 162).
- Respond in a timely fashion (within four days).
- Proofread your messages for typos, grammar, and organization of thoughts—even after you spell-check.
- Be appropriate as you would in a three-dimensional conversation. Converse to build relationships. Be as tactful and civil as you would be face-to-face in someone's office or living room.
- Be clear about whether your message is business or personal, or both. Earn the right to exchange personal and, perhaps, more intimate conversation.
- Use lower and upper case, as you would in a letter.
- Get permission before sending longer e-mails (more than a page).
- Follow up with people you said you'd e-mail.
- Like face-to-face exchanges, our e-mails should include and respond to:
  1. What was "said" to us
  2. The issue(s), projects, deals, meetings at hand.

Ignoring your e-mail, or changing the subject, does not contribute to the ongoing exchange known as conversation.

E-MAIL DON'TS: HOW TO AVOID BEING MO-DUMB

These are some cyber-don'ts unique to electronic conversations. *Don't:*

- Use obscenities. They read much worse than they sound.
- Send your three-page philosophy on anything—unsolicited.
- Use all upper case—that is taken as shouting.
- Send e-mail that could come back to haunt you, personally or professionally. (Think before you click "Send.")
- Use your office computer for "tricky" e-mail. If it's a business conversation, save the flirting, coming on, ranting and/or raving for a different time, venue, or modality. Issues of privacy, authorship, and work time should all be considered when using your office computer.
- Get caught in the send-reply-send syndrome . . . it can be a time waster. Indicate an end by signing off: "10-4" or "Over and Out."

SHARP CURVES ON THE SUPERHIGHWAY

Cyberspace is not without its dangers. Press the wrong key, and your gaffe may be a global one. Everyone in your database may get a message intended for only one person.

Remember that on-line conversations in the workplace, on company time, are not always private. The elite who delete may still face defeat, because e-mail can be undeleted and return, like Frankenstein with or without bride, to haunt us. Worse yet, to hunt us.

In *Being Digital,* Nicholas Negroponte, founder of the Massachusetts Institute of Technology's Media Lab, discusses the advantages and disadvantages of e-mail. One of the disadvantages may be the very ones that attract some of us: the lack of visual or verbal cues. We can't see the smiles, the frowns, the rolling eyes, or the intimacy created by "leaning into" the conversation. Nor can we hear the playfulness, charm, anguish, despair, enthusiasm, or empathy.

E-mail overload can also be a problem. The marketing director of a major firm told me his boss is so overwhelmed by the number of e-mails he receives that he doesn't even look at them! Be sure not to add to someone else's overload—and double-check via phone to see that important messages have been received.

"SMILEYS"

Emoticons—emot-icons or "smileys," as they are affectionately called—are supposed to help solve e-mail's "no affect" problem. They are a series of punctuation marks and abbreviations to let others know what emotions accompanied what was "said." They give us hints, but don't really compare with seeing someone's eyes light up and hearing the laughter we inspired. They can't capture voice inflections or body mannerisms—but we should know about these smileys and use them as well as we can.

Here are a few of them (courtesy of Dave Arnold, Infosight). Most of them are read by rotating the book clockwise 90 degrees.

SMILEYS

:-) Smile; happy	:-o Surprised; shocked
;-) Wink	:-# My lips are sealed
:-(Frowning; sad	8-) I'm wearing glasses
:'-(Crying	{:-) I'm wearing a toupee

—DAVE ARNOLD, INFOSIGHT

Abbreviations are also used. These include:

<g>	grin	BTW	By the way
LOL	Laughing out loud	IMO	In my opinion
ROTFL	Rolling on the floor laughing	IMHO	In my humble opinion
AKA	Also known as	OTOH	On the other hand

TYPE OUTCAST

The speed of electronic conversation can be a virtue and a problem. If we don't give a quick read for errors, we can convey additional (subliminal) messages that:

1. We are keyboard klutzes.
2. We don't proofread our work.
3. We are careless.
4. We don't have a grasp of the language or its rules.
5. We can't spell.

Remember: Spell-check doesn't. It doesn't check context, so you can wind up with phrases like "The pubic is

150

invited," as Jean Van Kirk's colleague discovered on a flyer for a fund-raiser for a school run by nuns.

Also remember: Be careful about humor on-line. Much of our humor is conveyed in tone, inflection, and expression. In print, well-meaning comments may be misconstrued.

ON-LINE SCHMOOZE: THE RESPONSE TIME OF OUR LIVES

Does all e-mail deserve answers? It's a judgment call. Some may not require a response, while others may need just a simple click or:

- "Great hearing from you."
- "The meeting time has been changed."
- "Thanks for the lead (update, data, etc.)."
- "Won't be in town that week."

CHAT ROOMS, FORUMS, AND OTHER GROUP GATHERING PLACES

Meeting strangers can be easier on-line because when we visit chat rooms and areas of special interest, we already know what we have in common with our fellow cyber-conversationalists. I've dropped into Speakernet to learn, listen, and exchange information with my professional speaker colleagues from the National Speakers Association.

Joan Eisenstodt is in a writer's forum on the East Coast. "There was a foundation of support and rapport established among some of the women, and some of us were happy to shed our anonymity," she said. "We wanted to

151

meet this great group of on-line friends, so we planned a day in New York City and it was fabulous. It further solidified our group by adding the personal, face-to-face dimension."

The Well, an on-line service out of Sausalito, California, has had face-to-face mixers for its members. On New Year's Eve, they held a party in San Francisco that was also on-line so people could celebrate multidimensionally.

The various chat rooms of the electronic cottage are the front porches of yesteryear—but not every chat room is a literary salon. According to Robert Rossney, "On-Line" columnist of the *San Francisco Chronicle* (November 2, 1995, p. E-5), "even great wits find it hard to say anything insightful or entertaining in a couple of typed lines. Most of us know how to talk; typing is another matter."

He suggests that chat rooms aren't always places for the best conversation, but "they are places to *find* people you might want to have a conversation with. Those should take place privately, in private chat rooms or instant messages."

LOGGING ON WITH A LATTE

Wayne Gregori, founder of sfnet in San Francisco, has found a way to combine face-to-face and on-line conversation by wiring two dozen Bay Area coffeehouses with text-only terminals. Many believe that the recent proliferation of coffee bars and cafés is less about espressos and lattes than about people coming together in person to brew conversation and percolate ideas. But some of these people also feel the need to chat electronically. In Wayne's wired cafés, "People can log on for a quarter for five minutes or pay a monthly fee to do research, join discussion groups, or check e-mail."

Wayne is a techno-savvy Renaissance man who is fluent in French and Italian and lived in Paris. "It was my fascination with language that prompted me to start sfnet. I wanted to offer people a way to communicate and to exchange ideas that was affordable. It also allows people to reexamine the way they speak and to relearn to communicate effectively. It's a community of people who meet regularly to discuss ideas, issues, and events.

"Sfnet is the 'parlor' or 'salon' of today. I've seen wallflowers blossom, as well as romances. We get to know one another as people, not as potential romantic objects. So many people feel—and are—isolated that being on-line provides a sense of belonging to this community."

Because Wayne realizes that social skills are honed in real space, he plans "netgets"—monthly gatherings at various coffeehouses.

"We have a gentleman who logged on daily and his contributions were brilliant," Wayne says. "His knowledge of a vast array of subjects was the talk of the group, and many young people were in awe of Alistair. One day we had a netget in Berkeley and in walked an older man who was tattered and dirty. People were uncomfortable with him. When he went up to each group and put out his hand, people thought he was bumming change. But what he said as he shook hands was, 'Hello, I'm Alistair.'" The collective cyber-mouth dropped.

"Alistair's on-line friends reacted emotionally. When he left, several people began to cry and the conversation moved to the issue of homelessness—as did the on-line discussions for months. Several people asked Alistair how this could happen to such a knowledgeable person. Alistair's reply was that he fell through the cracks because the information he knew was, in and of itself, not valuable. The lessons are still being learned by our net community because homelessness has been personalized by Alistair.

"One of the benefits is that friendships have been forged irrespective of our obvious differences," Wayne added.

WORLD WIDE WEB WONDERS

The www.com is full of information, but browsing the Web can put us on information overload—so Bob Rosin develops software for major telecommunications networks and is a Web master. Bob is in his third decade of e-mail, and suggests we be careful to avoid overload by finding good ways to choose what's valuable. There's a new guide published every week.

"My conversion to the World Wide Web came in 1995 when the doctor told me I had thyroid cancer," Bob says. "After telling Rosalie, my wife, I went right to the computer and typed in those ominous key words. I ended up in the National Cancer Institute and in a minute had the valuable research information I needed."

I became part of the Web last year, and am now a "site for sore eyes" (susanroane.com). I knew it was not the wave of the future, but the wave of *now,* and provides a resource for clients who want to hire me, too. Do I have a clue how my computer friend and expert Ken Braly constructed my Web pages? Absolutely not. I sent him my press kit, books, and audiotapes. I edited the first draft and voilà! It is another way to communicate in someone else's language and make ourselves understood.

HMOOZING VS. SOLICITING

...or of On-Line Marketing, provides a
...r those who don't want to incur the
...ans who police cyberspace.

...there is a vast difference between
..., purposeful chitchat) and solic-
...'atant invitation to do business."
...r. The latter could inspire oth-
...riate. She suggests that sar-
..., be avoided—and advises
...es, contribute information,

...g lets us forge business relation-
shi, ...t not have developed otherwise, but out-
righ, ...itation can be a turnoff.

THE NET EFFECT

We all need the skills to cyber-chat and "work the net"—
and this information is available in books, courses at local
colleges, and in on-line Help sections.

We nontechnocrats may need practice and a buddy to
find our way around. It's wonderful to have a patient
tutor who can explain, teach, and mentor us on flash ses-
sions, attaching files, and private chat rooms so we can
exchange information, ideas, leads, and contacts.

Will the Internet do away with our need to meet, mix,
and mingle in person? Absolutely not. We will still have
office holiday parties, client-sponsored hospitality suites,
fund-raisers, board meetings, cousins' weddings, family
reunions, and Christmas gatherings. And those face-to-
face events will require the congeniality, courtesy, and

conversational prowess that we can take back with us when we go on-line again.

REMINDERS

- **Relationships run companies and technology enhances those relationships. Conversing on-line adds another dimension to communication that can be beneficial and fun.**
- **On-line banter has a code of behavior known as "netiquette"—which we must learn and follow.**
- **We can mingle via modem, e-mail, chat rooms, and postings. But remember that social skills are finely honed in real time.**
- **Electronic mail has "flattened" the hierarchy of organizations.**
- **While this allows for open communication, be sure your messages are appropriate.**
- **Follow e-mail do's and don'ts to keep conversation open and flowing.**
- **On-line courtesy requires that we respond to the subject of the discussion, as well as contributing our ideas, questions, and thoughts.**
- **Observe the rules of the road when cruising the information superhighway.**
- **Spell-check doesn't, so we need to proofread our musings.**
- **Cyberspace is a great place to meet, learn, research, and exchange ideas, but conversing appropriately on-line requires common sense and civility. Being well-behaved on-line can serve us personally and professionally.**
- **Marketing on-line is best done by chatting purposefully (schmoozing), not by solicitations, advertisements, or sales pitches.**

CHAPTER 10

TALK TARGETS: BECOMING A MAGNET

Talk Targets are people with whom it is easy to make conversation. If you compliment someone on their conversational prowess and they look at you aghast, saying, "But I only talk easily and say clever things around you!"—then you are a *Talk Target.*

Being a *Talk Target* who makes other people brilliant conversationalists is an art—but one that we can all learn. These people offer, motivate, and encourage communication that builds relationships and business. We find them at work, at home, on sports fields, in meetings or classrooms, everywhere we go.

This chapter is about their secrets—and how they put their gift to work for them.

THE MAGIC WORDS

Talk Targets use certain magic words again and again, each time with sincerity and genuine connection. Some of the arrows in their conversational quivers are:

- "Please."
- "Your tie is great."
- "That's a great catch!"
- "How are you doing?"
- "Thank you."
- "Oops! I forgot."
- "You played a great game (round, match, set)."
- "I'm proud of you."
- "Excuse me."
- "How may I help?"
- "Congratulations on landing the client."
- "So sorry." Or "I do apologize."
- "Have a good weekend."
- "No, thank you."
- "How are you?" (Warning: listen to the answer.)
- "Good morning."
- "Good idea."
- "May I?"
- "Would it work for you?"
- "Would you be so kind as to return my call?"
- "Wow! That's fantastic."
- "No problem."
- "I could use your help."
- "It's my pleasure."
- "Good presentation."
- "Great job."
- "I'd be happy to."
- "How did it go?"
- "I have confidence you can do this."
- "How kind of you to offer."
- "You must be pleased (proud, happy)."

Recognize them? They're all words that show courtesy, respect, and consideration for others. There is no underestimating the effect of these magic words. We learned them early in life, and they are even more important now.

We spend millions of dollars a year on training and retraining, seminars on managing and motivating so that people can work harder, better, and smarter. Research has shown that what people really want is to *be acknowledged and feel appreciated.* We could save a lot of money just by making the magic words (*please* and *thank you*) part of our conversation cache. Try it. The responses may surprise and please you, and motivate you to use the magic words even more often.

Being polite and respectful is never a waste of time; it is an investment. I never heard anyone say, "My boss is such a jerk; he complimented me on my project design."

It may sound simplistic, but it is "the little things in life that count" and contribute to the conversations of life.

T. KAY-ODE

Not using the magic words consistently can cost more than we know. Dr. Kay was an assistant school superintendent of personnel. Six months after he replaced a well-liked administrator, one of his secretarial staff told me, "Dr. Kay never thanks anyone for anything. Whatever we do goes unnoticed."

A mutual associate wanted Dr. Kay to succeed, not to be sabotaged by his staff, so he shared the comment. Dr. Kay's response was, "Why should I thank them for doing what is in their job description?" No wonder his employees all thought they had "thankless jobs"!

Dr. Kay wasn't shy; he had plenty to say to colleagues and to the people whose votes he needed for projects, for funding, and for his contract. But his stay in the San Francisco Unified School District was short-lived. An educator with a Ph.D. in Human Resources should have known better.

TALK TARGETS "SALE" ALONG

It's easy to buy from and do business with Talk Targets.

Lee is a senior consultant with a major consulting firm that serves Fortune 100 companies. A few years ago, he finally landed an appointment with the chief financial officer of a big firm. "I had been warned that this guy was a 'tough hombre,' a man of few words who liked to get right to the point. That made me a bit uncomfortable, but I saw a photo of a beautiful boat on his desk and so I asked if he sailed. He said yes, and asked if I did. 'I wish I did,' I said, 'but I parasail and am sporting a bruise from my last outing.' He asked how it happened, so I told him and said, 'Let me show you.'"

The "tough hombre" relaxed, chatted easily about sailing, and ultimately gave Lee his business. Lee had hit upon a topic of importance to his client, and was willing to risk sharing and showing of bruises.

Lee is a *Talk Target* who used the OAR approach to maneuver what could have been rough waters. He:

- **O**bserved the photo.
- **A**sked about it with interest.
- **R**evealed his own sport and his bruises from it.

Lee also gave his potential client some information to which the man could respond. That built the conversation that gave Lee the business. What if Lee had changed his style of conversation to adapt to the "tough hombre" of few words? He may or may not have landed the client, but he would not have established the rapport that has made their business arrangement a pleasant relationship.

Bonnie Raitt's Grammy Award–winning song was right. As Talk Targets, let's give them "Something to Talk About." If we give people information on which to hang their conversation, they feel good about themselves and about us. My speech coach Dawne Bernhardt says, "I don't wait. When I say my name I add something the other person can hook into to build a conversation.

THE HEART OF SALES

The best salespeople are almost always Talk Targets because, as more and more people are discovering, *sales is conversation*—whether in the local jewelry store, shoe repair, card shop, specialty shop, bakery, boutique, or florist.

My former local compact disc store, City Discs, was owned by Chris Kimball, a young entrepreneur who is affable, open, smiles, and is a genuine Talk Target. He sold me six new CDs to enhance my environment while writing this book.

When I asked Chris if his ability to converse with customers was part of his sales success, he replied, **"Conversation isn't PART of a retail sale; it is the HEART of it."**

Chris listens to his customers, gets to know them, and recommends new and appropriate music. He also listens to his staff. A young employee is a ballroom and swing dancer who suggested he play a Perry Como CD. This, in the age of 10,000 Maniacs and Nine Inch Nails. But Chris did—and they sold five in a two-and-a-half-hour period! Moreover, the music created conversation and sales of other CDs. It made me smile, sing along, and tap my toes. (I love Perry Como.)

Talk Targets listen—and they get us to listen and talk as well.

Terry Norton, another Talk Target and co-owner of an upscale frame shop, concurs that conversation with customers is critical to success. "That's how we learn about our customers so we can meet their needs. By the time I have designed the framing for their family portrait, I can recite their favorite family legends and name both sets of grandparents. My clients, because they have been treated well and listened to, walk out of my gallery as my least expensive marketing tool—an enthusiastic referral. You can project any image you choose in a business conversation, but if you are insincere you risk being perceived as a phony."

"We are what we pretend to be."
—KURT VONNEGUT, JR.

Talk Targets observe people and assess situations to see what will make for the most enjoyable and productive conversations. If those Talk Targets happen to be in sales, they are bound to succeed.

FIT TO BE TIED

Talk Targets go out of their way to make people feel comfortable. Woody Morcott is CEO of Dana Corporation, a $7.5 billion company with factories in twenty-nine countries. At the cocktail hour before my program for his senior executives, I saw his fun tie and commented on it being so lighthearted and different. "Susan, because I am the CEO of Dana, some people may be uncomfortable approaching me. This tie is so eye-catching and fun that it lets people know it's okay to approach me. It gives them something to talk about, and also gives them a chance to feel good about initiating the conversation."

In the years since, more men are wearing Disney, Looney Tunes, Nicole Miller (the one with Butterfingers, Milk Duds, and Button Candy is my favorite), and other fun ties. They are conversation openers—and one of the few fashion options open to men in the corporate world. When we see someone with an unusual or fun tie, they are inviting conversation. It's okay to comment.

Women can invite people's conversation, too, with anything that is fun, bright, or unusual—a brooch, a dramatic chapeau, a lapel pin, earrings, or brightly colored scarf. The message we are giving is, "I am approachable." International speaker Patricia Fripp often wears stunning, dramatic hats that invite comment.

At a California Judges' Association reception, one of the retired judges was wearing a beautiful tie. My host turned to him and said, "Judge, that is beautiful—and I know because you are wearing it that you want me to talk to you." The judge then regaled us with the story behind the tie—it was a rendition of a Picasso from an art museum's special exhibit—and we had a good time learning something.

"Conversational T-shirts" are the latest ice-melters. Formerly the property of the underwear department, they are now personal statements. We wear our opinions, ideas, and commitments emblazoned on our chests. People buy them for us as gifts, or we get them as "part of the event." In either case, they give others something to talk about. My newest, *"Gimme Chocolate and Nobody Gets Hurt,"* is telltale. I also wear ones from the Chicago Art Institute's Monet exhibit, the Grand Ole Opry, King Crimson, and Robert Fripp.

TELEPHONE TALK TARGETS

There is a special sub-category of Talk Targets who make conversation easy, *even on the phone.* These people are doubly blessed.

Over the phone, our voices have to do double duty, communicating facial expression and body language as well as tone. The best telephone Talk Targets are easy, confident conversationalists who never come off as scripted, even if they are making a sales call. They are experts at the cold call—calling someone we don't know in order to make a sale—but their secrets for connection and success apply to all calls, both business and personal.

To engage people on the phone, we have to treat them as if we already know them and share a bit of ourselves to give them information on which to build. The catch is that we can't be presumptuous, and must be respectful.

THE ENORMOUS BENEFITS
OF BEING A TELEPHONE TALK TARGET

- Get and give information
- Connect with a contact
- Develop rapport
- Build business
- Learn something
- Solve problems
- Make a friend

The "You Never Know" School of Marketing applies to telephone conversations as well. Eight and a half years ago, I gave a program for the University of Hawaii at Manoa and someone suggested that I call Marcie Bannon, then a meeting planner for the National Association of Professional Insurance Agents. I did, and over two to three years we developed a telephone friendship and eventually worked together and met. Our enduring, loving relationship began as a short phone chat and has grown to a decade-long friendship.

Melinda Henning of Doing Business By Phone™ suggests that we prepare an upbeat message just in case we get voice mail. Give some piece of information that will make your call different, convey energy, and give the recipient "something to talk about" when the call is returned. Whether as a message or in person, these are the kinds of phone introductions that give people a hook on which to hang their conversation:

- "Hello, this is Arleen Honda from stormy San Francisco."
- "Hello, this is Carla Elkins from sunny Marin County."
- "Hello, this is Peter Skov from 49er country."
- "Hello, this is Ted Turner from the land of the free and the home of the Braves."

Weather and sports always give people something to which they can respond.

Telephone Talk Targets may be affable, but they get their business done. After pleasantries and connection, they move the conversation to business with phrases like:

- "Before I forget . . ."
- "May I change the subject for a moment?"
- "Let me just get back to the issue."

Talk Targets can also hear other people's exit cues—a lull in the conversation, papers being shuffled or the keyboard being used in the background, or a shifting or drifting voice. They take the cue with phrases like, "Thanks for your time, I know you're busy. Take care. Good-bye."

A WORD TO THE "PHONE-WISE"

Many people consider it their mission in life to circumvent the "gatekeeper," the person who answers and screens an important person's calls. They make these gatekeepers their adversaries and try their best to elude them.

Telephone Talk Targets *never* do this. Instead, they make friends with the gatekeepers. They become Targets for the gatekeepers' talk, and so they never have to worry about getting through. They are the gatekeepers' friends, and often enjoy preferential treatment—which impresses the important person as well!

TALK TARGETS MAKE IT SAFE

We can only build in-depth conversation when people trust us. They must feel safe in order to share deeper, more important, and more intimate thoughts, ideas, goals, and plans—whether the conversation is personal or professional. They need to know that their confidence won't be betrayed or misused. That trust, over time, builds the relationship.

If we are the ones sharing confidences, we should be careful about the "I am truthful, I tell all, I let it all hang out" school of sharing. When we are "in our truth," we may be taking care of ourselves at the expense of others—using them as "dump sites" or unpaid therapists.

This can be just as off-putting as people who share little about themselves. We need to take our cues from the others, honor their boundaries, and not spill our guts if it doesn't feel completely appropriate.

Dr. Judith Briles, author of *GenderTraps,* suggests that we monitor how much of our personal life we share at work, and refrain from telling too much, too soon. The informer fertilizes, fuels, and fires up the flames of sabotage, which can make our careers go up in smoke.

Cynthia Hanson, journalist and my walking partner in Chicago, says that good conversationalists don't delve into subjects that make us uncomfortable. An old friend resurfaced in Cynthia's life and regaled her with stories of her evenings in bars and her sexual encounters. It made Cynthia ill at ease. "I was not comfortable telling her that this was not my business, but she never paid attention to my cues." Talk Targets pick up cues and clues, because they pay attention to what people are *not* saying as well as what they *are* saying.

Daniel Goleman says in *Emotional Intelligence* that Talk Targets have well-developed social skills, empathy, and engage us in subjects that interest us.

EXPRESSIONS OF GRIEF

Talk Targets know what to say in difficult situations. It is sometimes hard to have a conversation with a person in crisis or mourning—but it's important to express support, sympathy, and concern, and perhaps to give them a gentle sympathetic touch. *Not* to do so "speaks" volumes about us, and doesn't say positive things.

I recently bumped into a former classmate whom I hadn't seen in a year and whose best friend had been senselessly killed in an act of terrorism in Jerusalem. "My best friend since we were toddlers is gone," Sharon said. "I feel like I lost part of me. It hurts; I am depressed."

I touched her outer upper arm and said, "You've suffered a great loss, a best friend. I am so sorry to hear of her death. This must be so heartbreaking for you."

We give our sympathies and condolences to families of those who have passed away, but we often forget the friends, who are often the "family of choice" and experience at least as much grief.

"I didn't say anything because I didn't know what to say" doesn't cut it. People have told me that they have felt ignored or abandoned by friends and colleagues who "didn't know what to say," so they said and did nothing. *We have to take the focus off ourselves and place it onto the person who is in pain.* This requires empathy and sympathy, even if we can only say, "I just don't know what to say, but my thoughts are with you." Remember, even bosses and supervisors lose spouses, siblings, offspring, and parents.

Even when we honestly feel too overwhelmed to respond to people who have experienced an accident, illness, operation, or death, there is a greeting card for every occasion. We can at least let people know we are thinking of them, and we may get an idea of what to say from perusing the cards.

EXPRESSIONS OF GRIEF

- "I'm so sorry to hear of your loss."
- "It's so difficult to lose a good friend (parent, spouse, child)."
- "I can't imagine it."
- "Please accept my sympathies."
- "How may I help?"

We don't have to say much, but we do have to be sincere. Sometimes the greatest gift is just listening to the bereaved with our eyes, ears, and heart. "It is so wonderful when someone shares a fond remembrance," said my friend Sylvia Cherezian, whose husband passed away. "The death makes you feel numb and as if your loved ones never existed. Those fond memories and stories confirm that they did, and are so soothing."

Being a Talk Target requires emotional intelligence, even in difficult times. People appreciate our empathy, and know when it is real.

THE MANTRA OF MODERATION

At the heart of Talk Targets' success is their ability to maintain balance. Anything can be a problem when taken to the extreme. The ability to balance and moderate our conversations shows up in many ways. These are some of the paradoxes Talk Targets have mastered:

- Being open, but not too open.
- Being silent to listen, but not too silent.
- Being sympathetic, but not gushy.
- Being of good energy, without overwhelming people.
- Being a talker and teller of stories without monopolizing the conversation.

Knowing what to say, and when and how to say it, is crucial. We can develop these skills by taking the time to be attuned to others. That is the secret of Talk Targets' success.

INCONTROVERTIBLE TALK TIPS

What do Talk Targets do to make others feel comfortable and encourage conversation? Here is a partial list, developed from my survey of ConverSensations:

- Take the first step and initiate. Say hello.
- Listen to introductions. Good listening requires practice and sometimes silence.
- Maintain eye contact and smile.
- Use humor appropriately to lighten conversation.
- Consider what is said and address it. Let the situation set the agenda.
- Be well-read and familiar with current events.
- Have a broad range of topics of interest.
- Encourage others to contribute.
- Volley the conversation by answering questions with a comment and a "return question."
- Learn about the perspectives and background of other parties.
- Shake hands web-to-web.
- Converse with an aura of authority and expertise.
- Ask the opinions of others.
- Tell interesting stories.
- Be open to change and exchange.
- Be enthusiastic.
- Use others' names in conversation.
- Refrain from monopolizing conversation.
- Use varied tones, inflections, and pacing.
- Pay attention to what has been said, and respond accordingly.
- Put people at ease with friendliness.
- Open up the circle of conversation by physically stepping back and allowing people to join.

We all do these things, but we can be conscious of doing more of them to be on our best behavior as confident conversationalists—and inspire others to do the same. That will make us Talk Targets in any group.

REMINDERS

- **Talk Targets have unfailing good manners, and make liberal use of magic words and phrases like "Please," "Thank you," "Excuse me," and "Congratulations!"**
- **Conversation is the heart of retail sales.**
- **Ice-melters spark conversation (fun ties, T-shirts, earrings, etc.).**
- **Talk to those in grief; express sympathy and share fond memories.**
- **Treat the telephone as a friend that links us to others. Think about why you are calling and be prepared. Don't sound scripted, even if you have a sales call plan.**
- **Talk Targets are always conscious of making it easy and comfortable for others to talk.**

CHAPTER 11

CONVERSATION KILLERS: WHAT *NOT* TO SAY

It's just as important to know what *not* to say as it is to know what to say and how to say it.

It's easier to recognize these conversational don'ts in others than it is to see them in ourselves—and we all need to assess our conversational strategies, patterns, and quirks against these conversation killers. Successful conversationalists who make us feel comfortable do not engage in these inappropriate behaviors.

> *"Speech is a God-given boon, peculiar to man, and must NOT be employed for that which is degrading."*
>
> —MAIMONIDES

DON'T SPEAK TO COMPETE

Conversation is not a competition nor a contest.

A group of us recently attended a "posh do," as a young English friend called the event. At cocktails before the bash, I watched and listened to our group. My escort and I were the "new kids." It was fun for me to observe the preening and verbal strutting, like male peacocks displaying their plumage and checking each other out. They actually reminded me of rappers—bragging, blasting, and blaspheming—with a subtler style, but the same message: Mine's Bigger and Better Than Yours!

Mine is a world of business, publishing, and entrepreneurship. I have heard colleagues wax rhapsodic about consulting contracts, clients, multiple speaking engagements, and book advances. In the telling and retelling, somehow the figures, perks, and benefits are always exponentially increased. An experienced friend once told me, "When you listen to these guys, just knock off a zero!"

A woman sales executive told me that competing about money was "the way of the business world. It's always about money; that's how many men define themselves. Because it's their measuring stick, it's a topic of conversation as a means to compete. In fairness, some women speak competitively about things, too."

DOWN WITH ONE-UPMANSHIP

Among genuinely successful people, our attempts at one-upmanship can quickly turn into one-downmanship. The first cousin to showing off, one-upmanship diminishes us as well as the person we're trying to cut down, and is clearly a conversation killer.

We need to be careful not to rain on anyone's parade. An associate told me, "One time when I had just returned from vacation in Hawaii, a colleague asked me which islands I have visited. When I told him, he waved his hand as if to dismiss those 'low rent' islands and proceeded to go on about the far superior islands where he 'frequently vacations.' It wasn't much fun, and I didn't feel like continuing the conversation."

Another competitive strategy—switching subjects in an untimely, inappropriate manner—also kills conversation. If a person isn't "doing very well" on one topic of conversation, he may change the subject suddenly to ground where he feels more confident.

Conversations should have a noncompete clause.

BRAIN BULLIES

People compete in many different ways. In some sets, the competition is about who *knows* more, who is more current, and who is best read.

A friend told me, "My uncle reads the paper first and I swear he memorizes it. Then he brings up current events and foreign affairs to show just how much he knows." *Gotcha!* is a competitive game, not a conversational skill. We read to create conversation, not kill it.

175

Nor is conversation necessarily a debate. The ability to reason and use logic is invaluable, and it's great to utilize critical thinking skills in formal debate—but it isn't always appropriate to good conversation. We will always have differences of opinion, but there are ways to handle them that don't result in debate. Some people think debate *sparks* conversation, but not everybody wants to play that way.

Good conversation honors our differences. A healthy discussion is not an argument. Having sparkle, not sparks, is the goal of interesting, informative, flowing verbal exchange.

INSTRUCTION IS OBSTRUCTION

Pedagogical diatribes are not conversation. "I am the teacher, the learned person who will tell you all you need to know" is not an attitude that makes conversation flow. Nor is "Let me tell you what to do and how to do it."

We all know people who must explain, instruct, or teach whenever they speak—and their conversation isn't very stimulating. Their speech is peppered with "you ought's" and "you should's." These phrases are dead give-aways . . . to deadly conversation.

Admittedly, I have had more than my share of "teaching conversations"—but I do try to monitor my "should's" and "ought's"! Eating one's own words can be so distasteful, but instruction is not nourishing conversation.

RoAne's Recommended Alternative: People who have wonderful information, processes, and expertise to share can always find an appropriate format: Offer to give a course at the local community college, volunteer with youth groups, or tutor in the schools.

CORRECTIONS OFFICERS

The grammar, syntax, and punctuation police can kill a conversation . . . mid-sentence.

A family friend from Chicago told me that her mother does this all the time. "It doesn't matter who's around or how many people are in the conversation. She interrupts and corrects me, and then expects that I say it the right way, her way, and just continue on as if nothing had happened. As far as I am concerned, it's rude. I am a big girl now—over fifty!—and she was never given my permission to be my personal grammar guru."

Whether the grammar police are trying to show off, put others down, or control the direction of the talk, *corrections kill conversations.*

OLD RULES, GOOD RULES

Some rules stand the test of time. One is that we don't discuss money in polite conversation. People who have had money for a long time don't discuss it at all.

Many people grew up with the dictum: "Don't talk about religion or politics." Others grew up in families that talked about little else. Now that we're adults, and on our way to becoming ConverSensations, we can use our own good judgment about when these subjects are appropriate—and when they are not.

The best guideline is the oldest rule, the Golden Rule: "Do unto others as you would have them do unto you." We want people to be considerate of our feelings, and not discuss subjects they know will make us uncomfortable. We should do the same unto them.

STRETCHING THE TRUTH

When we stretch the truth to impress, we usually get found out sooner or later—and create quite the opposite impression.

Jack A. thought he was coming across as Mr. GotBucks when he told two colleagues and me, "I slapped a bill [$100] on the counter and told the salesman to wrap that tie."

I was stunned, because I'd been in the store with him and knew he'd received thirty dollars change. His version was not only inaccurate, but the picture of him throwing his money on the counter and ordering salespeople around made him seem rude and ill-mannered.

How we treat service people speaks volumes about us—and so does our ability to speak the truth.

CONVERSATION IS NOT INTERROGATION

There is an art to asking questions. Like Baby Bear's porridge in "Goldilocks and the Three Bears," our tone has to be "just right."

That means not too probing, not too personal, not too aggressive, not too close-ended, not too open-ended, and *not too many* of them!

Remember, we are talking about *conversing,* not a game of Twenty Questions. When I hear a barrage of questions, my antennae go up. I get suspicious of the grand (or not so grand) inquisitor's motives. My neighbor Eva Nieto's remedy: She volleys the same question back to the questioner.

Over dinner with colleagues, I observed an "interrogation" of our East Coast visitor, a torrent of personal, probing, prying questions that made me squirm. The charm of the interrogator notwithstanding, this line of questioning was far too personal for the situation, which had a business component.

Though the person being probed was visibly uncomfortable being "grilled," he responded graciously to questions that were none of our business. He could have dealt with the interrogator by smiling and saying, "Oh, that's ancient history. I am far more interested in hearing about your (new job, car, computer, vacation, mountain climbing expedition, sales plan)." Moreover, our colleague, the charming interrogator, controlled the evening and prevented a four-way conversation from taking place.

Curiosity is a wonderful trait, but in excess, it becomes prying.

AVOID A PROBE-LEM

Beth described an evening with an ex-beau who hadn't learned that interrogation is not conversation. "I hesitate to return his calls because the last two times I was with him were a snooze. He spent the entire evening talking about his business and his oral surgery! He never expressed the slightest interest in me or my business. When I finally interjected an issue that was plaguing me, he bore down on me—asking probing, confrontational questions as if he were playing psychiatrist or FBI interrogator, trying to get me to expose my core."

Beth had just come back from Italy and told me she wanted to study Italian. So I asked her if that might not have been a better way to spend her evening than in the company of the boring ex-beau—and she agreed it would. Sometimes we just need to excuse ourselves from conversing with conversation killers and invest our time more wisely.

The other side of this issue is that we do want to show interest in other people, and questions are a good way to do so. "No questions asked" can be just as grating as too many questions. After three years, I realized that one former fan and new "friend" never showed much interest in my life. Although I knew everything about her, she knew very little about me. In a phone visit with another friend, I talked about this but said in her defense, "To Pat's credit, she doesn't pry."

My wise friend Marcie Bannon asked, "Susan, what makes you think that is good? After three years, a friend should know something about your past and your life. Maybe it's not that she doesn't pry, but that she's not interested."

No questions, no answers, no interest—and no real conversation. Balance and sensitivity are the keys to asking questions, and making sure that our questions imply no judgment.

SALES PITCHED

Have you ever attended an event (chamber of commerce mixer, professional association monthly meeting, or networking hour) and started to chat with "Mr. or Ms. Sales Pitch"? You know who I mean. Those people who are under the mistaken impression that one should always give a prepared thirty-second *commercial*.

Picture this. I was at a San Francisco Chamber of Commerce mixer, mingling as you would expect, when I happened upon a young man at the buffet table and said hello. He enthusiastically began to espouse his product line. I listened politely and asked some questions about his business, being a generous conversationalist, until he did the unpardonable. He asked if I "would like to have youthful skin." Geez! I thought I did! He then claimed he had the "perfect product to help me achieve a youthful look."

I smiled, gritted my teeth, grabbed his arm with one hand, pointed to my face with the other and said, "You see this face? It's been on this planet for forty-eight years. Obviously, I'm doing something right!"

The self-promoting commercial or sales pitch should be just that—pitched! Save it for an appropriate format, perhaps a structured networking event where everybody is asked to talk about their wares. **Conversation is not a sales pitch,** especially if it involves elixirs of youth—and aging skin.

Certain sales programs espouse a "probing question" methodology, but we need to be sensitive to people's reactions. If we're at an event to connect as people, and we're hawking our wares, we create an extremely negative impression.

THE SOLILOQUY BELONGS IN SHAKESPEARE

If you are not Shakespeare, keep the monologues and soliloquies in check.

I once had a business dinner with Gary Nongallant, an avid deliverer of soliloquies who tried to impress this author of *How to Work a Room®* by telling me he *really* knew how to work a room. "Twenty-five percent of the people don't like me, but when I leave a room, there is a void." What he may not have realized was that many people were probably grateful for it!

One day my friend Jeanie and I bumped into him. We were exchanging pleasantries about the American Booksellers Association convention, but then Gary launched into a ten-minute diatribe about his work, his business, his clients—name-dropping publishers with a vengeance. I finally interjected that Jeanie has been in the industry, but this got no response from him. When Mr. Void paused briefly for air, Jean and I said our good-byes and walked away. She turned to me and asked, "Who was that?"

Gary never asked a question of either of us, and made no attempt at anything that resembled a conversation. Jeanie had a client in his field, which she managed to mention at one point. If he had shut his mouth and listened, he would not have blown this lead from her. I had mentioned that I was writing this book, giving him a topic to bounce off of, but he had lacked the *interest* to inquire about it.

My friend Jeff Slutsky, super-speaker and author, shared a friend's "Five-Minute Rule": "If she speaks to a person who does not in the first five minutes ask a question or otherwise express interest in her, she exits."

Conversation is not soliloquy, and most of us aren't Hamlet.

A FUNNY BONE TO PICK

Some people's entire conversation is a barrage of jokes. "Did you hear the one about the . . . ?"

A client told me she worked with a fellow whose joke repertoire was enormous, catalogued, and committed to memory. I asked her if he was a good conversationalist and her response was, "I just know he is funny. Come to think of it, there's not much conversation with him. He mostly tells jokes."

The ability to tell jokes is a gift. It can be part of conversation, but it can't replace the give-and-take of real social exchange. If done excessively, joke telling becomes a monologue. That can be a way to control the conversation, and distance ourselves from the genuine involvement and dialogue that is at the root of conversation. **Remember, conversation is no joking matter.**

CONVERSATION IS NOT UNSOLICITED ADVICE

Remember the famous words, "This is for your own good"? It rarely ever is.

Spare me the people who ask, "Have you thought about . . . (losing weight, hiring an assistant, buying a Pentium, working with an etiquette specialist, coloring your hair)?"

"Gray hair is God's graffiti."

—BILL COSBY

Professional speaker Scott McKain told me of an incident at our National Speakers Association convention. "I was having an intense conversation with a longtime colleague about a mutual friend who had passed away. One of the attendees 'strolls into' our conversation and interrupts it by asking me a professional question, which I answered honestly and stated the results of the project were not what I had anticipated. I turned back to my conversation and this guy interrupts again to tell me I 'had given my power away.'"

Scott explained to him that he "had been honest, and that does not constitute giving power away." The "adviser" proceeded to give Scott more unsolicited, unwanted and unnecessary "advice," and Scott told the man clearly what he thought: "Who asked you in the first place?"

As my friend Lana Teplick has said for three decades, "Honesty can be used as a guise for brutality."

Unsolicited advice is almost always for the benefit of the adviser, not the advised—and it doesn't make for *good* conversation. Sometimes our work requires us to give advice, but we need to do it in the appropriate setting, and under appropriate circumstances. Emotionally intelligent conversationalists have honed the skill of giving advice in the right way, at the right time.

They understand that **conversation is not unsolicited advice.**

"DOIN' THE DOZENS": GOSSIP, RUMOR, AND "DISSING"

One person's gossip is another person's "shared news"— and I admit that sometimes I subscribe to the Alice Roosevelt Longworth school of conversation: "If you have nothing nice to say, sit by me."

But in truth, sharing information and news is dicey. One must be very careful not to:

- Bad-mouth other people.
- Start or pass rumors.
- Pass on negative information, even when it is confirmed as fact.

"Doin' the Dozens" is a street term for a verbal game of put-downs. My students in Chicago used to talk about and "do the dozens!" If memory serves correctly, this game was often initiated with the phrase "Yo Momma . . ."

But as adults, diminishing others does not demonstrate superiority. It just shows a lack of conversational skill, compounded by a lack of self-confidence and savvy.

People who are self-confident and comfortable in their own skin do not put others down as a means of building themselves up.

In fairness, some people are so used to thinking negatively that they don't even know they have been inappropriate. During a recent visit to Chicago, I brought pictures of me at the Black and White Ball, the biennial San Francisco Symphony fund-raiser. Prior to the ball, I worked out once or twice a day, monitored my eating habits, and lost 3 percent of my body fat. The goal had been to wear the "dream" dress, purchased three years earlier but never worn—and I did!

My Aunt Bertie went on and on about the photos. "This dress is fabulous! You look gorgeous!" she exclaimed. Two minutes later, she looked at the photo, looked at me, paused and said, "Susan, this doesn't even look like you!"

Okay. She meant no harm, and has been saying these kinds of things for nine decades. Can you change your eighty-three-year-old aunt? Maybe not, but in *Tongue Fu!* Sam Horn offers many ideas and strategies to deal with "the dozens."

In most instances, we can use "I" messages to let the transgressor know our reaction. How else can we expect them to change? One of her suggestions is that instead of using the word "but," which sounds like a criticism, use the word "and": "The manuscript was excellent but required copyediting" is better phrased as "The manuscript was excellent and required some copyediting."

The caveat for those who choose to put down, often using humor as a camouflage, is: You never know when you'll run into someone who is better at it than you are. The clever comeback may be your karmic come-around!

Conversation is not built upon put-downs, and "dissing" others is not conversation.

CAN THE *KVETCHING*

Some people complain incessantly, and this is all they are willing to offer or contribute. We all know them.

- "The service was terrible."
- "The car is a lemon."
- "The elevator is too slow (too crowded, too fast)."
- "The food was bland (too spicy)."

It doesn't matter what is said to assuage them; *kvetching* is their conversational M.O.—*of which we need no "mo!"*

We all have tales of what was so superb about a restaurant, hotel, photo lab, printer, or leasing company. It's not that we can't ever mention problems, as long as we limit our complaints and mix them with a healthy dose of curiosity, compliments, information, humor, and support.

DETAILS AT 11:00

Conversation is easily stymied by minutiae, the details that don't enhance a story or make a point. In a word, details that are *boring.*

Nobody is too important to remember details when it comes to business: meeting times, agendas, associates' names, the fine points of a contract, performance reviews, and project deadlines. But telling every detail of a story can result in overkill.

We need to know that Diane is in the hospital for an appendectomy, but we don't need a ninety-minute description of each cut the surgeon made. We may find it interesting and informative to go around the table at our professional association lunch and get a two-minute career summary from everyone, but the guy who takes a half hour to recite the responsibilities of every job he's held since age fifteen will put the whole table to sleep. We may need to know that the building project is on schedule and on target, but we don't need to be read transcripts of every conversation with the contractor.

We need to make sure our stories and comments contain only those details that are relevant, interesting, or have a point—unless we have a pal who also enjoys details. Again, it's a question of "feeling people out" and doing the right thing with the right person. I remember coming home each day after teaching and "sharing my day" with my then-husband, Griggs RoAne, who invariably said, "Get to the point. What's the bottom line?"

After too many times, my stock answer was, "That's why I call Syl [Sylvia Cherezian]. *She listens to the details, to the whole issue* and can stop me and advise me when I may have gone wrong."

Gender research in communications indicates that women are more likely to give details and listen to them than men are. Deborah Tannen stated in *Talking from 9 to 5* that this is a generalization. Some men give, honor, and listen to details—and some women don't.

Unless we're careful, **minutiae can mangle conversation.**

FINISHING TOUCHES

Conversation is not about finishing people's sentences. I remember one specific "conversation" in which an acquaintance kept finishing *my* sentences instead of coming up with his *own*. It was like a Greek Chorus— and it certainly couldn't have been because I was talking too slowly. While some think that chiming in demonstrates active listening and agreement, I say: *Conversation is not about "sharing" sentences.* We all have to have our own.

Because of my enthusiastic nature, I have been known to *chime in* with a positive comment myself. In a recent conversation with a colleague, she had to say, "Susan, wait and let me finish." Whoa! You can bet I did, and will continue to work on avoiding this conversation killer behavior.

Caveat: After a certain age, some of us do forget words or lose our train of thought. As my friend Lana told me, "Since I turned fifty, I lost all my nouns!" If you remember, feel free to jump-start that train of thought. It shows you're listening, and we love those who listen!

THE MONOSYLLABIC CONVERSATION KILLER

Gary Cooper is dead! "Yep" and "Nope" are not conversation! Even if we are asked a yes/no question by someone who hasn't learned about open-ended questions, monosyllabic responses kill conversation.

It is difficult to chat with a person who hardly responds, so most people won't bother. This may work as a technique for having the other person end the conversation, but it can leave a memorable—a memorably *bad*—impression.

Monotones are the cousins of monosyllables, and can also kill a conversation. The good news is that they, too, can act as sleeping pills or encouragement to the other person to end the conversation. To keep people's interest, we need to vary our pitch, pace, volume, and tone.

THE SARCASM CHASM

Sarcasm may be okay if used with a light touch in humor, but as a dominant way of conversing it will not endear us to people or advance our careers.

Sarcastic communication tends to be confusing and not very pleasant. It always has an edge, and the listener is never sure when or how that edge will be turned in his or her direction. Those listeners may be friends, family, bosses, employees, or colleagues—and there is no point in alienating any of these people.

Sarcasm may have been cool and clever in college, but once we move into the workplace, it's just plain risky—and a conversation killer.

It's a good investment of time and energy to examine our own quirks and style to make sure we are not committing any of the cardinal conversation killers that arrest communication.

REMINDERS

Conversation Is Not:

- **Competition . . . about money, deals, "toys," knowledge, degrees, or anything else**
- **Showing off**
- **Lies**
- **One-upmanship**
- **Snobbery**
- **An interrogation or probe**
- **A debate**
- **A soliloquy**
- **A sales pitch**
- **A joke . . . or a barrage of them**
- **Unsolicited advice**
- **A lesson**
- **Gossip**
- **"Dissing"**
- *Kvetching*
- **Sharing sentences**
- **Bashing**
- **Monosyllabic**
- **Monotone**
- **Long-winded answers**
- **Switching subjects**
- **Sarcasm**

If we assess our conversation, avoid these killers, and develop ways to cope with those who commit them, we are well on our way to becoming ConverSensations.

CHAPTER 12

COPING WITH CONVERSATION KILLERS: END IT OR MEND IT

Before figuring out *how* to talk to a conversation killer, we must first decide whether or not we need to do so— and *why*.

This chapter is about making that choice, and what to do if we *must* stay.

END IT

Ending the conversation is always an option. Most of the people I surveyed said that they dealt with the braggart, show-off, or competitive person by excusing themselves and moving on—unless there was a good reason not to do so.

Let's face it. If someone is involved in the annoying, demeaning conversation killers discussed in the last chapter—and there is no particular reason for us to be talking to that person—it makes sense to disengage and leave.

We have to ask ourselves: "Is this conversation a good use of my time?" If the answer is no, let's be practical and graciously excuse ourselves. Life's too short to do otherwise.

At a party or gathering, we can say simply and politely, "I hope you enjoy the evening," and move on to another person or group. This lets us concentrate on the people with whom we do want to spend time, or those with whom we *must* spend time.

Think of "ending it" as a time- and aggravation-saving device. If we don't bow out of these conversations, we have no one to blame but ourselves.

MEND IT

There are some people to whom we must speak no matter how hard they try to kill the conversation. They may be bosses, board members or clients, relatives, employees, or co-workers. We've all mingled and conversed with these people at work, at social functions, and on committees. We may even live with them!

These people are a fact of life, but we can learn to mend conversations as quickly as they try to rip them apart. Many of these conversation killers aren't doing it deliberately, and are not even aware of the fatal flaws in their verbal flow. They don't intend to obstruct social intercourse; but unfortunately, intent isn't the issue.

Our job is to be prepared so that we're not at a loss for words, and can redirect and salvage the exchange. It's no fun to seethe silently and then, an hour or two later, think of the perfect response.

Successful conversationalists are prepared for anything, even conversation killers.

STICKS, STONES, AND WORDS CAN HURT

Sticks and stones may break our bones, but the chant from our childhood is wrong. Names, put-downs, and insults *do* hurt us. They aren't called cuts, digs, and biting remarks for nothing.

Five-year-old Shayne Skov told me on a visit to "Grandma Susan's" house that he didn't like his new preschool because "the boys were mean." To her credit, mom Terri validated his feelings and told him that names *do* hurt, but said that those boys "aren't important enough for you to care about what they say."

Research on gender and communication tells us that this "ritual male teasing" starts at a very early age. At five, Shayne may not be interested in research, but it bears mentioning here because some conversation-killing behavior by males is part of this ritual teasing among boys. If we are aware of this and choose to communicate through it, the pattern can be broken—and we can prevent those sticks, stones, and names from hurting us professionally and personally.

As a teacher, I saw and heard much verbal cruelty—in the faculty lunchroom as well as in the schoolyard. The adults got away with it because their banter and gossip were more subtle and insidious, but our principal, Duncan Hodel, asked me to speak to each class because the hearing kids were calling the hearing-impaired kids names, and he thought the ten-, eleven-, twelve-year-olds were mature enough to realize how hurtful and inappropriate their words were.

If they could understand this, then so can we—and so can the hurtful conversationalists around us.

BOUNDARIES: SET 'EM AND SAY 'EM

Griggs RoAne, my former husband, always said, "People will only get away with what you let them." It's absolutely true. People cannot honor our boundaries if we don't let them know clearly where those boundaries are.

If we aren't willing to put up with certain behaviors and types of conversation, then we need to tell people in no uncertain terms what is acceptable and what is not. Setting these boundaries is not only our right, it is our responsibility.

Our silence gives conversation killers passive permission to continue hurting feelings, self-esteem, or careers. If we don't make the people who transgress aware of their transgressions, they will assume it is okay. Why should they do otherwise?

We need to figure out for ourselves where the lines are, and communicate them directly. And remember, when you are responding to the conversation killer, *don't smile while making your comment.* Dr. Geraldine Alpert, a Marin County psychologist, says that a smile confuses the listener and gives a mixed message, making light of something that is serious and undermining what we say. When we are "retraining" people on how to speak, respond, and communicate with us, it's critical to give clear messages.

THE THREE Rs

We all need to be e-"quipped" with defenses against conversation killers. It makes sense to be prepared with several comments that you can use when necessary.

The essential Three Rs for coping with conversation killers are Remarks, Responses, and Retorts. We must have some of each in our repertoire (or arsenal), and be clear when to use which.

The Remark, according to *Webster's Unabridged Dictionary,* is "a comment, a casual observation or brief expression of opinion which implies special attention, note or judgment. Something remarkable is noteworthy. As a verb, to remark is to perceive." *Example:* "Harding Park, our local golf course, is so well-tended that it is lush green year-round."

The Response is "an answer or reply in words or actions. To respond (verb) is to reply." *Example:* "What's my age? When asked my age, I always tell the truth . . . give or take a few nanoseconds."

The Retort is a reply delivered in a sharp or retaliating way; a reply in kind. It turns the accusation or epithet back on the person who said it. According to *Webster's* second definition, it is "an incisive or witty reply." *Examples:* "It's none of your business," or "What would ever compel you to ask?"

These Three Rs are variations on a theme, and we must pay attention to how and when we use them.

ROYAL RESPONSES ... REALLY?

Remember, "It's not only what you say, but how you say it." That is why we have to be careful with written communications—especially when we're "retorting." The printed word can be tough to interpret because people can't see the smile, the lilt, and facial expressions, or hear the tone of our voice.

In 1995, Princess Di flew through San Francisco with her sons on her way to Vail for a holiday. When a fellow passenger casually asked, "Where are you headed?"

Princess Di's answer was, "Wouldn't you like to know?" Then she smiled and raised her eyebrows in a conspiratorial manner. Her tone was so pleasant that the United Airlines attendant who overheard this conversation interpreted it as a clever, witty remark—not a biting, sarcastic retort.

Our tone and manner often determine how people receive our remarks, responses, and retorts. Take the word *really*.

- Say it as a question. *"Really?"*
- As an adverb. "Really c*omplicated!"* or *"Really* complicated!"
- As an interjection. *"Really!"*

The same word sounds different and has a broad range of meanings, depending on how we say it. Each of the following comments can express several reactions, depending on how they are said:

- "Isn't that extraordinary?"
- "My word!"
- "It's hard to believe."
- "Aren't you the lucky one?"
- "How impressive!"
- "That's a thought."
- "Aren't I lucky to know that!"
- "Interesting."
- "Whatever made you think of that?"
- "Thank you for sharing!"

This last one is a favorite, and takes on a special twist here on the West Coast, where "sharing" was a frequent pastime in the 1970s and 1980s. It can be said with deep appreciation for a lovely comment or thought we've been told. Or, said differently, it's a great response to not-so-lovely comments. I've used it both ways.

Here are some remarks, responses, and retorts that may be appropriate when someone has been a verbal vampire—depending on the situation and what is at stake:

- "What compelled you to say that?"
- "What do you mean?"
- "I didn't need to know that."
- "I'm surprised (disappointed, displeased) to hear you say that."

We should have four to five standard comments with which to respond, remark, or retort to conversation killers—when it's appropriate.

GRACE UNDER FIRE

In certain situations, we need to stay above the battle rather than engaging conversation killers directly. With a few direct, well-chosen words, we can let our feelings be known without stooping to their level.

Customer service manager Chris Leech expressed his reaction to his brother's constant barrage of negative comments in such a loving way that the brother was able to hear him. He said, "I don't know why you make such negative comments. They hurt me. You are my role model and I look up to you. When you criticize me, I see myself poorly. It hurts and it is not behavior that I admire."

I "KID" YOU NOT

I "kid" you not. When I was married, people often asked me why we didn't have children. After a keynote speech in Las Vegas, I was seated with two attendees from the United Kingdom who had never heard a woman keynote speaker. At the dinner, one gent asked if I was married. I said yes, and he asked about my children. When I said I didn't have any, he felt compelled to ask why not—in a hostile tone that almost threw me for a loop. Miracle of miracles, an answer came to me that normally would have taken two to three hours. I replied in a quiet, slow-paced tone, with no smile, "Not everyone is so blessed."

He dropped that line of questioning quickly, because he did not want to hear any painful accounts of a personal nature—and we proceeded to a lighthearted group conversation that was appropriate and fun.

During one of my presentations, an audience member suggested a response for those hurtful, biting comments: "Ouch!" with a pained look. We all know what it means without engaging in a hostile interchange. *It delivers* the message that barbed comments are not welcome, and people usually get the word.

Barbara Nivala, Executive Vice President of the National Speakers Association, is the epitome of grace under fire. She accompanied me to a speech I was giving before an audience of local professionals sponsored by a major auto dealer. When we arrived, I introduced myself and Barbara to the owner of this magnificent dealership. He turned to me and, instead of saying "Hello" or "Welcome" or "We're happy to have you here," he said, "You got any of dem dar termaters [tomatoes]?"

I truly had no clue what he was talking about; I barely understood him. He asked me again, then turned and asked Barbara, "You got any of dem dar termaters?"

Finally I said, "I don't understand your question." He shrugged his shoulders, smiled sheepishly, pointed at me, and said to Barbara, "You know, termaters [tomatoes] to *throw* at her."

There is no accounting for bad taste, judgment, or humor. In this case, I was hamstrung because he was not only my client, but the client of the corporate auto headquarters and the speakers bureau who had hired me.

Barbara handled the situation with great grace and charm, saying, "No, we don't do that."

Sometimes silence is the most gracious answer. Gert Gurd is a former confidential secretary to a school superintendent and still volunteers at her local hospital. She has "been on the planet a few decades" and is convinced that "sometimes the unspoken word is the best thing you can say."

It's a judgment call based on the answer to the question my friend Lana Teplick always poses: "What would be the point?"

THE HIGH ROAD

We may have to take the high road with conversation killers in most business situations. But there are times when we must stand up for ourselves—even and especially with our bosses. Like the students I used to teach, some adults push us just to see where our edges are. They want us to set limits. Doormats get stepped on.

Jill's boss yelled, called people names, and threw tantrums. It created a very unhealthy environment, and everyone in the office all responded differently. Several people just ignored him. Others were cowed. Jill waited till the explosion subsided, then went into the office and told Ole Yeller that she realized he was upset, but she didn't appreciate his yelling and would prefer to be corrected in a civil manner. To her amazement, he listened and has tried to control his screaming, at least at her.

There is a risk involved in this approach. The boss may feel threatened, get angry, make your life miserable, and perhaps even get rid of you—but the proliferation of lawsuits, EEOC complaints, and violence in the workplace may inspire people to self-correct more readily.

SAVING FACE WITH GRACE

Allowing people to save face is a smart move. The best negotiators know that saving face is critical to success—and sometimes letting others save face is critical to our jobs. Some face-saving comments are:

- "That's a thought."
- "That's certainly another way to look at it."
- "While that doesn't work for me, it may serve others."

By letting people save face, we can often keep an argument from developing or escalating—and save others, and ourselves, from even worse behavior.

DEALING WITH THE OFF-COLOR AND OFF-TARGET

Some people feel compelled to put down and make fun of people from other groups—or to tell off-color jokes—in an effort to appear clever or hide their own discomfort.

I'm always surprised when people forget some of life's basic rules, because you never know who is listening:

BASIC RULES FOR LIVING AND SPEAKING

- Think before you speak.
- If you can't say anything nice, say nothing at all.
- Do unto others
  A. As you would have them do unto you—
     and/or
  B. As they would prefer to have done unto
     them (from *The Platinum Rule*, 1996, by
     Tony Alessandra, Ph.D.)

There are several ways to cope with a person who belittles others:

- *Say nothing* and glare, raise an eyebrow, or roll your eyes.
- *Pose a rhetorical question* like "Why would you say such a thing?"
- *Share your philosophy:* "I never find humor that is at the expense of others to be amusing."

It can be dicey when the group humor turns raunchy, insulting, or otherwise inappropriate. We all want to be part of the group, and a glare or making a face may or may not be enough to stop the inappropriate banter. Some women have said that men actually use off-color humor on purpose to "test," embarrass, or exclude them—but many men say that the raunchy jokes and stories offend them as well. Again, "you never know!"

The "I" message is usually best in these situations:

- "I don't like that."
- "I did not find that funny."
- "It makes me uncomfortable."
- "I think that is inappropriate."
- Or Grandma's favorite: *"Feh!"*

Foul language falls into the same category as group put-downs and off-color humor. Some people find it crude and offensive, and it backfires easily both professionally and personally.

A woman I know who is a charming communicator occasionally uses what she described as "salty" language. While conversing with a former client, who must have been on a "low-salt" diet, she said one of her "not so bad" words.

"There was dead silence. So I asked him if he was uncomfortable. His response was that he had heard the expression, just not from a woman. That caught my attention." She apologized and decided she would edit her comments in the future. To her credit, she picked up on his discomfort, apologized, and self-corrected.

HOW DARE YOU TALK WHILE I'M INTERRUPTING!

There are times when conversation killers have to be stopped before they kill again! One of those times is when they interrupt us during important presentations. Rude is one thing; destructive to our careers is another.

I'm not speaking of people who interject New York–style enthusiasm ("Great!" "Wow!" "That's exciting!"), which Dr. Deborah Tannen says in *That's Not What I Meant* need not be taken as interruptions. Those are only momentary interjections that punctuate our presentations, not *prevent* them. The people who must be stopped are those who interrupt, add their bit, and never bring the focus back to our point.

In meetings, we can cope with this conversation killer by being assertive and calmly saying, "I appreciate your point, but I want to finish my comments. Then you may continue."

Some other suggestions:

- "If I may continue."
- "I am not finished."
- "Let me finish my thought, and then you can have the floor."

This takes great courage and practice, but it is part of the verbal self-defense that contributes to the success of our careers. We need to have a planned, practiced commentary for these inauspicious occasions. If we let people interrupt us, others in positions to recommend or promote us may think we are pushovers who will not be heard among clients or competitors.

Statistically, men interrupt more than women—but some women do interrupt and some men do not.

COPING WITH THE SARCASTIC

One of the difficulties of coping with sarcastic people is that they often think they are more clever . . . than they are. Even people who appear to enjoy sarcasm are understandably wary of someone who's holding a verbal knife. This form of communication rarely suggests the joyful, or the positive, in life.

The best way to cope with sarcastic or caustic conversationalists is by using "I" messages such as:

- "I'm unclear what you are *really* trying to say."
- "It would be easier if you just said what you meant."
- "What exactly do you mean?"'

Bad habits are hard to break, and Sarcastic Sam may make another caustic comment as soon as you've said something. If no attempt to converse clearly is made, or the response is not positive, excuse yourself and move on. It's probably not worth your time and energy to stay. If you do need to talk to the person, just ignore the sarcasm and move through the conversation until you achieve your purpose. Or say something like: *"Would you please rephrase your comment so I am clear on its meaning?"*

Virginia Tooper founded Sarcastics Anonymous, and we all know who the members are.

COPING WITH THE QUESTION-ABLE QUESTION

Certain subjects are inappropriate in public, and others are inappropriate at any time. We need the skills to finesse these situations and redirect attention away from these questionable topics.

Conversation Killer: "How much were your commissions last quarter?"

Conversation Coper: "About what I expected them to be."

When asked to divulge business data, a colleague replies, "That is proprietary information." Then we can either volley the question back in a more appropriate way ("What does your company do to create incentive?") or change the subject: "Oh, by the way, I read that there's a marathon in Marin (a tennis tournament in Tallahassee, a jazz concert in Kalamazoo, or a new first baseman for the Baltimore Orioles)." Switch topics to the news, weather, sports, movies, the stock market, the supermarket or market-driven customer service. Anything. You get the drift.

Or else use the tried-and-true alternative: Excuse yourself and move on.

HEREIN "LIES" THE DIFFERENCE

People who speak what we know to be untruths aren't always telling intentional lies. Sometimes we perceive or remember events differently because we all have different "filters"—as was obvious in the famous duet between Maurice Chevalier and Hermione Gingold in *Gigi:*

> "We dined at 9:00."
> "No, it was 8:00."
> "I was on time."
> "No, you were late."
> "Ah yes . . . I remember it well."

And we often don't. But people who intentionally lie are problematic. What if we find ourselves in a conversation *à deux,* a social group, or a meeting and hear a colleague, co-worker, or relative say something that bears no resemblance to the facts as we know them?

Is silence the best coping strategy? Maybe. Again, it's a judgment call. The best "voice" to listen to is the one in our stomach; it will advise us wisely.

Another coping strategy is to open the possibility of alternative "truths" without making the speaker lose face. We can try phrases like:

- "That's not how I remember it . . ."
- "If my memory serves me correctly . . ."

Then we can give our version, if it's appropriate. As always, "I" messages work best. They prevent us from saying things that sound like "You are a liar."

It's always best to summarize meetings that generate actions, contracts, or agreements with a letter or memo. That makes for clarity, adjustment, and agreement. It helps keep us all on the same page, despite our filters and different perceptions, and enhances understanding. The extra investment of time is well worth it, if we prevent miscommunication.

Paul Ekman, author of *Telling Lies,* is a University of California at San Francisco psychology professor who specializes in lie detection. To detect lies, he says, we should learn to read micro expressions and gestures, as well as discrepancies between words and emotions. "We must [also] factor in how motivated you are to believe what you are hearing!" (*San Francisco Chronicle,* August 8, 1993)

When we hear lies or when our stomachs warn us that something is untrue or even just amiss, my advice is: STEER CLEAR. People who lie often *believe* their lies, and there's not much we can do about that.

"MELANCHOLY BABY" TALK

Some people are chronically depressed, or given to wide mood swings, temper tantrums, and other challenging behaviors. This is another case in which it's best to steer clear, if possible.

"Melancholy is an indulgence of the young."
—UNKNOWN

We all have our ups and downs, an occasional "bad hair day" or disappointment. But the person who does not bounce back, or continues to behave poorly and take it out on friends or co-workers may need a paid professional friend.

Lending our ear may be a nice, but insufficient gesture—and to do so on an ongoing basis may not be good for us or for them.

COPING WITH *KVETCHES*

Complaining is a way that people bond in the workplace (*Talking from 9 to 5,* Tannen), but it is a form of bonding that we should monitor—in ourselves and others.

Martha Dragovich, a speech/language pathologist in Vallejo, California, was at the end-of-the-year faculty party. One of her colleagues *kvetched* and moaned, as was his pattern, until she could listen no longer. Martha smiled and said in a tone laced with irony, "That's what I like about you. You are always so positive."

Perhaps he was unaware of how his constant complaining sounded—but Martha's comment must have been his epiphany. Since then Mr. Kvetch has looked for the positive and has upgraded his outlook. Addressing the issue can get great results, especially when people aren't aware of what they are doing.

We all come into contact with negative people—in the office, in the community, and in our extended family.

There is some "darkness" in everyone, but we need to be on the lookout for people who are so happy being miserable that they want to make the rest of us miserable as well. We don't help them or ourselves by "putting up with the situation." A comment like Martha's, or even one that is more direct, can work miracles.

The other side of this issue is remembering not to over-*kvetch* ourselves. Negative people rarely fare well as managers or team members because they have trouble inspiring and motivating others.

The first cousin to the *kvetcher* is the chronic critic. There is no pleasing this guy or gal. Judgment is at his core, and the chronic critic always finds something amiss.

When Sherwood Cummins was a Presbyterian minister with a parish, his church had a choir. "No matter what I did, the choir director had a criticism. I knew he didn't like me, but I continued to try to meet his expectations . . . unsuccessfully. One evening, a member of the choir came over and said, 'Don't waste your time trying to please someone who doesn't want to be pleased.' It was the best advice I received."

Like *kvetchers,* critics are sometimes unaware that they are either doing something negative or putting people off. A word to the wise ones often changes their behavior. If the behavior doesn't change, we need to reassess our relationship with them.

STOPPING THE NONSTOPPER

Conversation is impossible with monologists who hog the stage and never give others a chance to speak. To succeed in business and be nurtured in our personal lives, we need to avoid this behavior ourselves—and learn to stop those who won't stop it.

Susan Witkin Tandler, news radio commentator, has a solution: "When confronted with this type, I smile, tell them to shush, and that it's my turn. It usually works. If it doesn't work, I move on."

We may be tempted to say "a few choice words" less pleasant than Susan's, but it's best to take a deep breath and count to ten. If we have to interact with a nonstop talker, we need to let the person know that there is a problem. Again, many people are unaware that they are doing anything that impedes conversation, or their own success.

"By swallowing evil words unsaid, no one has ever harmed his stomach."
—SIR WINSTON CHURCHILL

For every conversation killer, there is a conversation thriller. I believe that most people want to be smooth, confident, comfortable, and interesting conversationalists. If we develop our skill at coping with and retraining the obtuse, off-base, and inappropriate, we will be doing both them and ourselves a favor. And we always have an option: If we can't MEND the conversation, we can END it—and move on to other more receptive, nice, interesting, energetic people who may be easy Talk Targets.

REMINDERS

- If there is no reason to continue a BAD conversation, BOW OUT.
- Set boundaries and state them; we teach people how to treat us.
- Use "I" messages: "I am uncomfortable with . . . (foul language, put-down humor)."
- Know the differences among responses, remarks, and retorts—and when to use them.
- Have four to five comments prepared so as not to be caught off guard.
- Silence is sometimes the best response.
- It is both what we say and how we say it; tone is telling.
- Curb foul stories and language—and don't put up with them if they become too offensive.
- Interrupt the interrupters.
- Pay attention to signals, and to the wise voice in our stomachs.

CHAPTER 13

HOW TO CONVERSE IN A DIVERSE WORLD AND WORKPLACE

To succeed in today's world and workplace, we must be comfortable exploring, addressing, and bridging diversity in nationality, culture, religion, race, gender, preferences, and capacities.

Conversation is how we do that. The better conversationalists we are, the easier it is to bridge those gaps and enjoy the diversity that is all around us.

It is good manners and good business to develop the skills to converse easily and appropriately with new acquaintances, friends, colleagues, clients, employees, and bosses who are different from us. If we don't have those skills, we may lose contracts, clients, staff support, a promotion, or a rich relationship.

THE DIVERSITY OF DIVERSITY

Technology is expanding the global workplace and making it multicultural. There are Hispanic, African-American, Asian-American chambers of commerce to provide resources, ideas, and networking opportunities among members. Many large corporations have networks of employees who meet to share resources, ideas, job leads, and support, as well as deal with company issues and policies that affect them. Professional associations abound that serve members of specific ethnic groups or gender: the Society of Women Engineers, the Society of Black Meeting Planners, Asian-American Journalists, among many others.

Technology is also making us a "blind" society because so much of our communication is by e-mail, voice mail, fax, or on the phone. The person on the other end of our communication may be very different from us—and he or she may be a colleague, a potential client, or even the person who signs our paycheck. It's more important than ever not to talk "down" to anyone. Patronizing patter is evident in tone and facial expression, as well as in words. It is unkind and unwise. Talk politely to people on all rungs of the ladder. Again, *you never know!*

In our diverse world and workplace, some people advocate focusing on our commonalities. Others espouse celebrating our differences. We don't always melt in the melting pot. While we do have common issues, we still retain our individual identities as Irish, Native American (Sioux, Apache, Shoshone), Argentine, Sicilian, Jewish (Reform, Conservative, or Orthodox), Japanese, Okinawan, Taiwanese, Buddhist, Methodist, Hispanic, Baptist, African-American, Catholic, or some combination of the above.

The best rule is to focus on our commonalities and celebrate our differences, because we bring both our similarities and differences to the workplace and the world. For my survey, I chose respondents who crossed ethnic, racial, cultural, and geographic boundaries and represented a wide range of ages, professions, and careers. Some were city folk, others farm folk. Very different, very diverse, but all had something to offer to the conversations of life.

People who can converse across cultural, religious, ethnic, and racial lines are, as John Marks, CEO of the San Francisco Convention and Visitors Bureau, says, "the real communicators who succeed."

PEOPLE FIRST

Regardless of our diverse affiliations, we are all people first, individuals whose behavior cannot be predicted simply because we belong to an "identifiable group." We bring our unique humanity to the workplace and to the banquet of banter. We also bring differing levels of tolerance and humor.

To illustrate this point, I share the story of a woman from Fresno, California, who vacationed alone in Las Vegas. She hit a huge jackpot, but didn't trust anyone else to count her winnings, so she decided to take the bucketful of silver dollars to her room to count them.

Shortly after she got on the elevator, three black men got on. She heard one of them say, "Hit the floor." Scared to death, she did precisely that. The silver dollars flew everywhere. From her position, facedown on the floor of the elevator, she heard loud, uncontrollable laughter. The three men were convulsed, but stopped laughing long enough to help her up. She got off at her floor and dashed to her room directly across from the elevator. Two hours later, there was a knock. The bellman handed her a vase of roses with $100 bills hanging from each flower. The note said, "Thank you for the best laugh ever. Eddie Murphy."

Because the woman had brought some prejudgment and stereotypical thinking to the banquet, and into the

213

elevator, she misinterpreted a command to press the elevator button for the right floor as a threat to her safety.

We are often confused about how to communicate and converse with people who are from different backgrounds from ours. Sharon Gangitano has studied and researched American multicultural studies from the perspectives of anthropology, sociology, and linguistics. Her advice, as an African-American woman, for conversing both professionally and socially with people of diverse backgrounds: *"Talk to people who are different than yourself as you would talk to those who are like yourself."* She also suggests that we make a conscious effort to keep from pigeonholing or stereotyping people.

A WORD TO THE WISE

How we cope, communicate, and behave with those who are different from us is a measure of our skill, values, and adaptability. It speaks volumes about us.

After a luncheon speech I gave for a national convention, Patricia came over to chat. She was charming, smart, and funny and had a very good position in consumer affairs in the travel industry. She was, incidentally, in a wheelchair. She asked, "Susan, would you please address the issue of mingling with those that are different? As long as we are sitting at the luncheon table, everything is fine and I am one of the gang. But as soon as lunch is over and I move my wheelchair, people get tongue-tied. I've been in this chair twenty-five years and am quite comfortable. I'm also a good conversationalist! Tell them that they can still have a great business or social chat with me—no matter what kind of chair I use."

I promised Patricia I would do that and, in this chapter, I keep my promise.

FOOD FOR THOUGHT-FUL COMMUNICATION

Don't avert your eyes and ignore those whose differences may cause discomfort. Initiate. Offer a smile or hello in the elevator, employee cafeteria, or at the cappuccino cart.

THE (ARETHA) FRANKLIN SOLUTION: R-E-S-P-E-C-T

Aretha is right. Respect should be the bottom line when relating to people we meet who are different from us. When we give our respect, our errors are forgiven. If we don't convey respect, our words are subverted by our tone, intent, and actions.

We all want to be treated with dignity—and the person we choose to ignore may be the potential client who could sign a big contract. Or the senior executive who hires, promotes, or refers us to a job or corporate board position.

To make sure we give respect where it is due, we need to ground ourselves in some conversation basics: communication, civility, and common sense.

BEING HUMAN

It's no weakness to show empathy. The emotionally intelligent are the ones who create harmony—in the workplace and in life.

Shorty Sneed and I met on a plane fifteen years ago. We stayed in touch for years, but then I didn't hear from him. He called recently to explain that the family had been through a difficult time. Shorty's nineteen-year-old daughter was in a car accident and is a quadriplegic. "She's an inspiration to me because of her spirit, determination, and outlook," he said.

Shorty told me that the tremendous outpouring of support and love from family, friends, and the community at large proved to him that people are basically good-hearted and well-intentioned. "Lori is back at Ole Miss finishing her senior year. I am so grateful to her friends who continue to involve and include her in their social life. Maybe some people said things that weren't the best; but I am pragmatic and I focus on the positive, so I only remember how wonderful everyone has been and continues to be. And Lori's sense of humor, personality, and good sense make her a delight to be around."

Both Shorty and Lori have learned a lot about how both friends and strangers treat people who are different. He told me, "One time in a restaurant the waiter asked me what Lori wanted to eat. I looked at him and said, 'Don't ask me, ask her.' Another time, a waiter raised his voice to ask my daughter for her order. She looked at him and said, 'You don't have to shout. I'm not deaf; I'm paralyzed.'" Lori Sneed is truly the comeback queen!

Shorty's advice: Don't look away. Say something. Small talk is good. Big talk will evolve. Lori has her spunk, spirit, and sparkle. Someday she will be someone's professor, wife, mother, or manager.

A friend and former client, Leigh Bohmfalk, echoes this advice: "Since my operation, I have met and talked to so many nice, interested people, because my cast creates conversation. It's a great excuse for people to approach me who are probably lonely and want to talk. I'll miss that cast—but I have learned a great lesson in disability awareness. Because people have been so open to me, I will never again avert my eyes from someone who is different."

CHAIR-ISHED ADVICE

After an operation, meeting planner extraordinaire Elizabeth Goulding had to spend several months in a wheelchair. "Oh! The lessons I've learned," she says. "Some people who know me well averted their gaze because I had screws and pins in my leg. I knew it was because they cared, but couldn't talk about it. I made it easier for my boss by making a joke so he could respond with humor.

"One of the things I would say to those who are differently abled is not to respond defensively to ordinary acts of kindness. Sometimes when a door is too heavy to push, I am delighted that someone has offered to open it. When it's a light door, I say, 'Thanks, I can do this.' Help isn't pity. Most people who are helpful are empathizing, and they shouldn't be rebuked. Their offer comes from goodness.

"In this country we don't know how to design for wheelchair traffic. In my town they redid the streets but didn't shave the sidewalks down to the level of the streets so there are huge bumps that are difficult for me to navigate. Everyone ought to have a day without an ability—in a wheelchair or with a blindfold. It would give each of us a rich perspective."

SOLUTIONS

We can make it easier to converse by:

- Listening more intently to the person whose speech pattern is different or accented, especially in the global workplace.
- Positioning ourselves physically to enhance conversation. We may have to create visual distance from someone in a wheelchair so that no one ends up with a pain in the neck.
- Speak with our faces as we articulate.

CORRECT INTERPRETATIONS

It's increasingly possible that our co-workers at all levels of business may be hearing-impaired—especially as the baby boomers age.

According to the *Wall Street Journal,* there are 84 million hearing-impaired workers in the United States. Although "they still face discrimination in the job market, the positive changes have been striking. The advent of faxes and e-mail, and the FCC's expansion of interstate relay service for text typewriters (TTY's), allows users to communicate through regular telephones with the help of an operator. Technology has leveled their playing field."

Lois Vieira is a resource teacher for the deaf/hard of hearing and instructor in total communication and sign language. She has observed numerous situations that called for a sign language interpreter. Her advice: "Make sure that we don't direct our conversation or eye contact to the interpreter and treat the person with whom we are speaking as a third party. When we focus on the interpreter, it is belittling."

This advice applies to both sign and foreign language translators. With our forays into global business, it is good advice.

A family-owned San Francisco company was run by several brothers, one of whom was hearing-impaired. Like many people of his generation, he went to the oral school and was never taught sign language. Research indicates that even the best of lip-readers barely and rarely catch even 50 percent of what is said. If this man were your boss, you would want to make sure that you were communicating as well as possible when engaging him in conversation. That means facing him when you speak, and enunciating your words.

Slight hearing loss is more common than we imagine. The baby boomers are turning fifty, and have listened to thirty-five years of rock and roll.

A CEO who was a Vietnam veteran told me he had a 30 percent hearing loss, so he watches faces as he hears words. Current research by Charissa Lansing on lip-readers at the University of Illinois indicates that some people who are profoundly hearing-impaired scan faces for information, looking at all areas of the face, not just the lips (University of Illinois, *Inside Illinois*, October 5, 1995).

Let's learn from the lip-readers, and speak with increased animation and expression to be better understood. It serves us well to remember these tips for being understood:

WHEN TALKING WITH HEARING-IMPAIRED

A Few Do's
- Enunciate, don't exaggerate.
- Animate words with expressions.
- Position yourself face-to-face.

A Few Don'ts
- Cover your mouth.
- Use your favorite poker face.
- Turn your back and talk.

WHEN WORDS DON'T WORK: LANGUAGE BARRIERS LIFTED

There are some people who understand, and make themselves understood, regardless of language fluency.

My aunt Milly Cohen is the best at this. Although she lived in Israel on and off for thirty years, she never became fluent in Hebrew. Yet she never had any trouble communicating with her Israeli and Arab neighbors and friends. Her daughter, Sheri, who was fluent in both French and Hebrew, found Milly's ability to converse without language fluency both humorous and irritating.

"In France I'd speak to people in French and they would look at me as if I were from another planet," Sheri says. "Mom would gesture, laugh, give a *universal* sign, inject a word or two of French, and the conversation would flow and become animated. To this day, she is still friends with several people we met in France who actually think she speaks French."

We converse with more than our words. Enough said!

(DON'T) SHOUT IT OUT!

We tend to shout at people who speak differently—as if the Russian, Chinese, or Spanish speaker will *understand* what we mean if we say it more loudly.

I learned about this firsthand during the month I had to be silent because of a vocal cord problem. People's reactions were varied. Many people assumed I was deaf, and spoke louder. Others spoke in "little sentences," as if I knew only rudimentary English. Surprisingly, a few knew some sign or finger spelling, and I had to let them know that I could hear even though I couldn't talk.

My silence was a remarkable time of introspection, lessons, and reflections—and it taught me that words are only a part of communication. (I also learned you can buy cousin Kayla her wedding gift without uttering a sound.)

DOWN UNDER... FEELING LIKE A SHRIMP ON THE BARBE

Even when we are fluent in a language, we must familiarize ourselves with the cultures and respect their ways. Before I went to Australia for a three-program, three-city tour to present "How to Work a Room," I read several books on customers, culture, and terminology. But I never could have anticipated my faux pas.

Before the part of the presentation where I get the

attendees to meet and mingle, I said, "You can't work a room on your *tush!*" The responses were snickers, raised eyebrows, and some laughter. I had thought that this Yiddish term would be familiar, because there is a Jewish population in Australia. It was, but it did not refer to our derrieres! It referred to an even more intimate part of our female anatomy, a word I would never say in public!

Who knew? This warning was not in the guidebooks. But people understand global gaffes, and the audience was forgiving. When my meeting planner explained what I had really said, I apologized to the audience and turned it into a "how *not* to work a room" lesson.

We can't ignore the culture and customs of others; we must know and respect them. We never want to be "Ugly Americans," even in the United States.

NOT LOSING SIGHT OF CONVERSATION

Having a conversation with someone who is visually impaired has always been easy for me. Perhaps it's because we can see the impairment, and know that people who are visually impaired often have great insight, information, and global vision.

One caution: We tend to speak more loudly around visually impaired people, and there is no need for this.

David Hand, a restaurant association executive who is partially sighted, enjoys a sense of humor about his sight: "I have offered to be the designated driver, but there are never any takers!"

BABY DOCS, ETC.

These days some fifty-year-olds are reporting to thirty-six-year-olds. It can be a bitter pill to swallow. In *Party of One*, a delightful cabaret show, one of the songs lamented that "my doctor is younger than I"—and so is the lawyer, the rabbi, and maybe even the boss. It's not an easy situation, but it can work if both parties embrace the richness and variety of experiences that their differences bring to the workplace.

Conversing across generational lines is a feature of managing change and honoring accomplishments. Ray Du Boise, a retired Bank of America vice president, filled me in on the highlights of his interesting career—from being a shy eighteen-year-old only child who entered the army and found sixty bunk mates in the "family," to being a retiree with three different careers behind him. Ray is a great believer in the relationships and the network one must have to maintain one's position and resources. "I could always pick up a phone and call a colleague or competitor, and get the information I need."

To Ray, the most memorable conversationalist is Walter Fulton, an eighty-two-year-old Bank of America executive who is still a consultant. "They hire him to go to the industry trade shows and conventions because he knows everyone, and opens the doors. He introduces the younger employees and gets the conversation going." Fortunately, some people at Bank of America are smart enough to know what they need and hire the person who fills that need regardless of age. It would behoove the staffers, colleagues, and competitors to make sure they converse with Walter. He still makes deals happen!

Most people are helpful, interested, interesting, and respond to those who are sincere. That cuts across racial, ethnic, gender, age, and cultural lines, and it applies to those both abled and differently abled.

"AGING" CONVERSATIONS

"Generational confusion" can creep into the conversation, whether the person to whom we are speaking is older than we are, or younger. Part of the "Generation X'er vs. Boomer" tension is a kind of parent-kid squabble transplanted into both the workplace and the popular culture.

Young managers and associates have often asked me how they can approach and talk to senior people in the industry or firm. Here are some ideas:

- Speak intergenerationally. Learning from those with more experience and those with differing experiences is still learning.
- Good manners make a great impression when speaking to an older, more experienced person.
- Use the person's title until they say otherwise.
- Focus on the event, project, or problem in common.
- Ask intelligent, open-ended questions. ("How has your membership in the CPA Society helped you?" "What was your oddest client experience?")
- Offer something about yourself. ("I never imagined that I would get to attend a conference with this many industry superstars.")

These tips apply not only to X'ers speaking to Boomers, but to Boomers speaking to the World War II generation—and to anyone speaking to an elder.

MAY/DECEMBER/MAY

If your client is significantly older or younger, treat him or her as a particular favorite. Most people have interests, hobbies, and lives outside the office: parents and children, obligations, music and movie preferences, alma maters, and geographic loyalties. Find out what these are and speak to them.

Again, the keys are respect, and making people feel comfortable with us. We can respect the experienced colleague who has longtime information about the industry (and may know where the bodies are buried). We can also respect the bright, young, energetic person who has a great education and highly developed computer skills.

There is no reason to speak arrogantly or rudely to either of these people, or in any way to convey an aura of superiority. One may not be able to get into his motherboard, but have a top sales record and a few tips to share. The other may ask "Shakespeare Who?" but devise an ingenious program for the database and get the whole office behind it in an afternoon. When these two people can work together, magic happens.

CONVERSING WITH KIDS—OF ALL AGES

Bottom line, the trick to dealing with people who are significantly older or younger is no trick; just be open, interested, and have respect. This "trick" works with anyone who is different.

Talking to senior or junior citizens is based on the same sound principle offered by Sharon Gangitano: "Talk to those of different ages than you are as you would talk to someone your own age—with the same tone, interest, and attitude."

Teachers and good managers know that people rise or fall to our expectation level. Expect the best, and you will probably get it.

When Simone Davalos, a Yale freshman, was a junior in a private San Francisco high school, she complained to her mother that a math tutor "talked to her like a teenager." Simone *was* a teenager, but her tutor did not understand Simone's depth, intelligence, and spirit. Finally, during the fourth tutoring session, the teacher began to talk to Simone as a person. She was delighted.

Kids are people. They have interests, ideas, and opinions. They need to do homework, make career plans, and get to ball games. They could be the boss's offspring, or a client's. It may be *your* child who attends a company picnic or holiday party, and is treated nicely and made to feel comfortable by a colleague, employee, or boss.

We don't forget such kindnesses—and neither do others.

DEALING WITH DIFFICULTY

Sometimes we face challenges that call on us for the highest level of empathy and communication. We spoke in Chapter 10 about expressions of grief to people who have suffered misfortune and suggested phrases like:

- "I don't know what to say."
- "I'm so sorry."
- "I can't imagine what you're going through."
- "Is there anything I can do?" (Then do something without being asked.)
- "I can't imagine how you must feel."

Another kind of difficulty, mental and emotional challenges, can also make people feel "different." Katie told me of her daughter's recent change of medication to counteract clinical depression, which had actually caused her condition to deteriorate to the point that her daughter had checked herself into a psychiatric facility. Trying to be positive, I responded by saying that was a good sign. Wrong words! Katie's look let me know before her words did that I had hit a nerve. "There is no good news, unless it's that she stops pulling this nonsense!" she angrily responded. Her words came from twelve years of pain and fear for her daughter's life.

Mental health issues are tough to talk about, but they do exist and they have an effect both in the workplace and in the world. Clinical depression, and its antidotes, are more common than we might believe—and the "right" words are difficult to choose.

I apologized to Katie and explained that I was just looking for the hope in the situation. She then told me of another friend who always knew what to say and how to say it. "Oh, dear, I'm so sorry. How can I help you?" the friend had asked.

DON'T ONE-UP ONE WHO IS DOWN

According to Lois Vieira, this is not the time to come up with a competing story that suggests, "If you think that's bad, I can go you one better." Researchers tell us that people do this in an attempt to control the conversation and avoid having to deal with emotional discomfort.

Art Berg, motivational speaker extraordinaire, is a quadriplegic. He says that his situation in no way diminishes the difficulties or traumas that befall others. We all go through our own issues, problems, and heartaches.

TAKE HEED, TAKE HEART

When someone is different from us, we need to remember the difference between our interest and our curiosity.

The person (or their parent, if it's about children) may

not have the time to give us a seminar about having triplets, children's hearing aids, or developing a degenerative disease. If we speak to them as we would speak to anyone else, everyone will be more at ease.

When Jeanette Bruciati and her son Michael were at a local shopping mall, a woman approached them and said, "Hi, Michael. How are you?"

Michael smiled, returned the hello and said, "Mom, I'd like you to meet my customer." Michael is friendly and comfortable with people who are friendly to him. He works as a bagger at the local supermarket where there is a dress code (white shirt and tie). Jeanette has noticed that management is not always consistent with the way they respond to Michael as an employee. His manager seems to have difficulty confronting Michael because of his disability (Down's syndrome) so Michael sometimes gets away with things like not observing the dress code. "I hope it is not because of Michael's disability, but I think it is."

Some advice for conversing with Michael from Jeanette Bruciati, which has a universal application:

- Talk to Michael the way you would talk to anyone else.
- Respect him as a person.
- Avoid inappropriate (childlike) teasing.
- Listen with your heart and your ears. If you don't understand something Michael says, just ask him to "tell me another way."

These heartfelt hints can help us like the person we see in the mirror better, and contribute to our self-image and confidence.

THE DON'TS: WHAT TO AVOID

When dealing with people who are different from us, we need to be sensitive, open, alert, and respectful—then say what comes from our hearts. But there are some words that almost never work. A few of them are:

- "Some of my best friends are . . ." Sharon Gangitano, my aerobics classmate, responds: "How interesting. Some of my best friends are, too."
- "You people ought to . . ." This makes the assumption that we are the experts and have the answers to racial, religious, or ethnic concerns.
- "What do you people want?" Shirley Davalos, video producer and co-owner of Orion Express, remembers hearing, "What is it that you Chicanos want?" on too many occasions. Shirley is lighthearted and one of the most calm and positive people I know. She would smile, shrug her shoulders, and say, "*All* of us! Gee, I couldn't say!"
- Don't tell a joke about the group to which a person belongs.
- If, for example, you're talking to an African-American, don't confine your talk to Michael Jordan or Shaquille O'Neal unless you are at a basketball game.

THE DO'S: WHAT TO DISCUSS

When we avoid the don'ts, anything else is a do, and fair game. Again, remember to pay attention and speak with respect. Without respect, anything can sound, and feel, and *be* patronizing.

Here are some topics that are safe to discuss with almost anyone:

- Your venue or location.
- The politician who is having the fund-raiser, the museum where the benefit is held, and so forth.
- Current events, sports, the organization sponsoring the event.
- Movies, weather, books.

MAGIC SOLUTIONS?

The real communicators who succeed in our diverse workplace convey their willingness and desire to make people comfortable with them—no matter what is happening in their lives. Those who endeavor to make people who are different feel comfortable have a gift that is boundless.

I wish I could provide a magic solution for society's ills. That may not be possible, but I do know that the ability to make successful conversation and put people at ease makes the world a better place. It also brings enormous personal and professional rewards. I hope this chapter makes it easier for you to talk to all kinds of people—but the most important thing is that I have kept my promise to Patricia.

REMINDERS

- The workplace is diverse in race, religion, ethnicity, age, culture, language, and physical ability—and the keys to communication are common courtesy and civility.
- The "melting pot" is a myth. We need to be aware and respectful of our differences as well as our commonalities.
- The secret of conversation with people who are different from us is to treat people with respect.
- Talk to people who are different the way you talk to people who are the same. Treat people who are different from you as if they were the same. Topics: the weather, the project, the boss, the new marketing plan, the event, the news.
- You never know! The person who is different may be a supervisor, potential employee, or client.
- Don't ignore or avert your eyes from people who are differently abled.
- Be open to people of different ages. There is much to learn from others.
- Most people are helpful, interesting, kind, and sincere.
- The benefits of being able to converse in a diverse world are incalculable and contribute to our professional and personal success.

CHAPTER 14

TEN COMMANDMENTS OF CONVERSATION

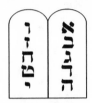

1. Thou shalt bring banter to the banquet of life.
2. Thou shalt prepare for conversation by being well-read (newspapers, journals, and books) and well-rounded.
3. Thou shalt pay attention and focus on others by making eye contact.
4. Thou shalt listen, listen, listen (with ears, eyes, face, heart). Empathize. Respond. Listen to learn; learn to listen.
5. Thou shalt be of good humor, avoiding put-downs at the expense of others.
6. Thou shalt shine the light on others.
7. Thou shalt be appropriate in jokes, words, stories, and behaviors.
8. Thou shalt engage others using an OAR (Observe, Ask, Reveal).
9. Thou shalt have a manner of speaking that exudes good manners, courtesy, and respect.
10. Thou shalt speak with people who are different as you would with those who are similar.

FOR THOSE
DESPERATELY SEEKING SUSAN

a speech is within your reach!

"Work" my Web site: **http://www.susanroane.com**

Snail mail	The RoAne Group
	320 Via Casitas, Suite 310
	Greenbrae, California 94904
Voice mail:	(415) 239-2224
Fax:	(415) 461-6172
E-mail:	SROANE2224 @aol.com
	75671.2056@compuserve.com
For books	1-800-358-3301
and audio books:	(Cheshire Cat Bookstore)

How to Work a^{TM} *Room*

The Secrets of Savvy Networking

235

Susan RoAne addresses corporate and association meetings, retreats, conferences, and rallies. Some of her clients include:

- Dana Corporation
- Hershey Food
- Monsanto Corporation
- Arthur Andersen
- Procter & Gamble
- Motorola
- Bank of America
- Infiniti
- Apple Computer
- Exxon Corporation
- Edward D. Jones
- Anheuser Busch
- Century 21
- Andersen Consulting
- Pacific Bell American
- Emst & Young
- KMPG-Peat Marwick
- Wells Fargo Bank
- LaSalle National Bank
- International Council of Shopping Centers
- American College of Surgeons
- University of Chicago School of Business

- AT&T
- Lucent Technologies
- GTE Hawaiian Telephone
- Citicorp
- National Football League
- Ohio Edison
- Waste Management of North America
- Price Waterhouse
- Bank of America
- Cartier Jewelers
- Discovery Toys
- Automobile Association
- National Restaurant Association
- Harvard University Alumni
- Managed Futures Association
- Associated General Contractors of America
- Professional Insurance Agents

APPENDIX

At-a-Glance Guide to Everyday Conversations: Talk Tips

REMINDERS

- Eighty-eight percent of us are shy. Being uncomfortable with strangers is normal.
- Give people the benefit of the doubt. (The quiet person may be shy, not a snob).
- Choose to Schmooze . . . practice everywhere.
- Read a daily newspaper.
- Most people feel good about being approached, being sought out.
- Listening is the key to conversation.
- Best opening lines: Big smile, firm handshake, and "Hi!" or "Hello!"
- People tell us what they want to talk about. Listen closely.
- Have a planned self-introduction keyed to the event, giving a benefit (e.g., at the Restaurant Association, "Hi! I'm Peter Piper in the pickled pepper business," or "I help people spice up their meals without the garlic aftertaste").
- Bring your OAR to build conversation (Observe, Ask, Reveal).
- Maintain eye contact while conversing.
- Verbal Fluency = Affluence and Success!

GUIDE TO SUCCESSFUL CONVERSATIONS: A "CHAT" SHEET

THE EVENT

(Fund-raiser, swim meet, graduation, wedding)

Smile and make eye contact. When we do so we become approachable.

Greeting

Shy Person: "Hi!" or "Hello!" (90 percent of us will respond in kind.)

Un-shy Person: "I'm Brian Palmer from Chicago Bulls Country," extending hand for handshake. (Brian has added information to build on.)

Response

Shy Person: "I'm James Washburn."

Un-shy Person: "I'm James Washburn. What do you think of Michael Jordan's new contract?" (He picked up Brian's extra information, made an observation, and asked a relevant question.)

Response

Shy Person: "Amazing."

Un-shy Person: "It's amazing that someone can have so

many zeroes really add up . . . and he's worth it . . . for the team, the city's presence, and the economy. Are you a sports fan?"

Response

Shy Person:	"No."
Un-shy Person:	"Not really. I am an antique car collector."

To Do:

- Add some information to make it easier to converse with you.
- Talk about the venue, the event, the location, or even the weather!

Not to Do:

- Ignore the comments made . . . as they are the gems for generating conversation.

Listening and responding draws people into an exchange. Interest is the cornerstone of interesting!

THE BUSINESS EVENT

Whether it is a meeting, trade show, conference, hospitality suite, keynote address, we are missing opportunities if we are not conversing.

A Big to Do

Smile and make eye contact.

Greeting

Un-shy Person: "Hi! I'm Melody Lingerson from Lima."

Response

Shy Person: "Hi, I'm Jesse James."
Un-shy Person: "I'm Jesse James. Are you from Lima, Ohio, or Peru?"

Response

Shy Person: "Ohio."
Un-shy Person: "Oh. I am from Ohio, but would love to visit Peru. Have you?"

Response

Shy Person: "Yes."
Un-shy Person: "Oh, yes . . . it is a beautiful country. I was in Machu Picchu."

Response

Shy Person: "Oh."
Un-shy Person: "Did you climb it before it became so commercialized?"

Response

Shy Person: "Yes."
Un-shy Person: "Yes, it was in '85, splendid and not commercial. Speaking of commercials, I see by your name tag you are with Betty Bloopers Beepers. What is it you do?"

Response

Shy Person: "I own a business."
Un-shy Person: "Some days . . . too much . . . I am the founder."

Response

Options: "How old is the company?"
               or
          "What inspired you?"
               or
          "I have a friend in the personal beeper market; we went to college together. His name is Burl Covan."

Response

Shy Person: "Oh."
Un-shy Person: "Sure, I know him. Great guy. He helped me edit my first brochure."

To Do:

- Have a prepared self-introduction of seven to nine seconds that is linked to the event.
- Give a benefit or comment that engages.

Not to Do:

- Answer in monosyllables.
- Ignore or be aloof to people who are being friendly. You never know!

By giving information, listening to responses, and offering a comment or question, we build the foundation and structure of conversation.

THE BUSINESS EVENT WITH SPOUSES

Caution: We must treat spouses with respect, interest, and regard. Sometimes the member is female and the spouse is male. This is a tricky issue, as many spouses choose to stay home with children and are embarrassed by the unfortunate social stigma. Let's avoid contributing to the discomfort.

Greeting

"What do you do?" is NOT the optimum opener.

"What do you do in your spare time?"
   or
"What do you do in your leisure time?" are better, because they allow for a wider range of responses.

"I recognize you from a prior retreat. Do forgive me. I cannot pull your name from my memory bank."

"How many of these conventions have you attended? What is your favorite venue? Speaker?"

For the participant:

"Which special places do you plan on visiting while you are in San Francisco?" (or: "What seminars will you attend?")

For a colleague's spouse:

"You must be Marcia's husband. I've heard about your screenplay. It is a joy working with Marcia on our team."

For the spouse who is not salaried, a response to "What do you do?"

"Oh, I have a twenty-four-hour-a-day job where I am on call seven days a week—and don't need to wear a beeper."

To Do:

• Speak to spouses with interest and respect.

Not to Do:

• Ignore spouses at events or dismiss them as unimportant.

Remember, spouses can have an enormous influence on business decisions, and have interests in arts, sports, charities, movies, and business.

FUND-RAISER (A TRUE STORY)

The OAR method helps us converse while we traverse smooth and not-so-smooth waters. And, the sincere compliment as a conversation opener builds the exchange, positive memories . . . and votes!

Let's give people "something to talk about," like a tie, hat, pin, earrings, tie tack, sweatshirt.

Notice anything that is unusual, different, attractive and give a compliment.

Cheryl M. wore a frog pin on her lapel when attending a fund-raiser with President Clinton.

O. The President noticed the pin and said, "What a lovely frog pin!"
A. "Did you know I collected frogs?" continued the President.
   CM (Un-shy): "Really? How did you start?"
   Shy Person: "No."
R. President: "My daddy used to say . . ."

Not a long exchange, but attentive, focused, and engaging, built on an observation and compliment.

To Do:

- Realize there is a common thread upon which to base conversations: the cause for the fund-raiser.
- Notice "conversation starters."
- Compliment . . . when it is sincere.

Not to Do:

- Forget to mix conversations, questions and revelations . . . the magic is in the mix.

THE FUNERAL, WAKE, OR MEMORIAL

It is important that we pay our respects in such difficult situations and are respectful when we do so.

What to Say (With a touch on a hand or arm)

"I don't know what to say. My thoughts are with you."
or
"This is such a loss. Ned was such a special person."
Pause for the response and share a remembrance:

"I remember when we were both assigned to the same project and used to wait for the supervisor to return from coffee . . . and one day . . . Ned got impatient . . ."

What Not to Say

"You're young; you'll remarry."

"That was some casket . . . must have set you back a pretty penny." (*Oy vay!*)

On the loss of a child (life's great tragedy): "The Lord wanted little Johnny with him."

What to Do or Say if Someone Utters the Above Words

"If you will excuse me" and move away.

"Ouch."

"Pardon me?" with a quizzical look.
 or
Just ignore it . . . as the unintentionally hurtful person is ignorant.

THE WEDDING OR SOCIAL EVENT

Smile and make eye contact. This is a joyous occasion.

Un-shy Wedding Guest: "Hi! I'm Ruthe Hirsch. Are you a friend of the bride or groom?"

Options:　　　　　　　"Isn't this lovely?"
　　　　　　　　　　　　 or
　　　　　　　　　　　　"Have you been to a wedding at the Caprice before?"
　　　　　　　　　　　　 or
　　　　　　　　　　　　"I heard the band before at a bar mitzvah; all of us danced into the night."

Response (to first question)

Shy Person:　　　　　"Neither."
Un-shy Person:　　　　"I'm Greta Garbled, the date of the stepfather of one of the bridesmaids."

Response

Un-shy person: "Which bridesmaid?"

Response

Un-shy person: "Oh, the redhead. She and her stepfather remained close after her mother and he divorced . . . especially after her natural father died. So, he knows the bride very well."

Ruthe: "She looks lovely. How nice to have a stepfather who is so special and stays connected in this day and age when we hear of so much bitterness."

Response

Un-shy Person: "Oh, yes, she and her brother are quite close to him. Let me introduce you to him."

Giving more information allows someone who is listening to build upon it.

To Do:

- Remember, these are festive occasions; life's celebrations.
- Have fun!

Not to Do:

- Overindulge in drink . . . especially if the social event involves business associates.

NAME GAME

We meet so many people that it is difficult and unrealistic to expect to remember everyone's name.

What to Do

Take the initiative and always stick out your hand and say your name as you shake hands. Ninety percent of all people will respond by doing the same . . . then no one struggles to remember names.

Do Not Say

"I've met you at the last three fund-raisers."
If someone has said this, and you have not remembered them . . .

A Response

"How nice of you to have remembered my name! You have a terrific memory and I would love to know your memory secret."
   or
"Do forgive me. I can't remember your name. It seems my memory bank is closed to withdrawals."

What Not to Say (especially to older people)

"Hello. Do you remember me?"
or
"It's nice to see you" (without adding your name).

To Do:

- Reintroduce yourself clearly saying your name.
- Ask for the correct pronunciation if you are not sure how to say a difficult name.

Not to Do:

- Chastise or embarrass someone who has a memory lapse regarding your name.

If someone forgets your name, be gracious. We all forget from time to time, and our graciousness speaks volumes and builds bridges and conversations.

EXITING REMARKS...REMARKABLE EXITS (FROM THE NONSTOP TALKER, BRAGGART, OR BORE)

To Do:

Wait until you are saying something and interrupt yourself
... and excuse yourself by saying (in a positive tone):

"I hope you enjoy the rest of the party (conference, game, seminar, etc.)."

and walk one quarter of the room away to another group, person, or buffet.

Caveat: The person we perceive as boring may just be shy and uncomfortable until we have hit on a subject of interest.

Shy and formerly shy people are great conversation partners, as their eyes don't roam and they are in the moment. All of us have interests, avocations, information, and knowledge. The chance encounter . . . of the You Never Know School of Marketing could be the bonus banter of a lifetime!

Not to Do:

Look around the room or over the shoulder of your conversation partner for someone more interesting, with a better title, more attractive.

What to do and say if someone is "surveying the crowd." Follow their glance and ask in an upbeat voice:

"What is it?"

It could be the arrival of the guests of honor . . . or just catching someone being rude.

Pay attention to people, surroundings, and events.

FOR SUCCESSFUL CONVERSATIONS

Be involved.

What we observe, hear, and read is fuel for fabulous conversations.

Listen and eavesdrop. Material for conversations is everywhere . . . in bookstores, movie theaters, health clubs, bleachers, coffee salons, comedy clubs, the classroom, on the television, in our families, and . . . in Congress!

YIDDISH GLOSSARY

The following are some Yiddish terms I've used in the book, plus others that you may know and find useful and/or amusing. I thought you would enjoy these definitions as modified from Leo Rosten's *The Joys of Yiddish*.

Bris "The Covenant"; a ritual circumcision ceremony observed on the boy's eighth day of life.
"At Ari Tandler's *bris* even I got squeamish when the *mohel* picked up the instruments."

Chutzpah *Classic usage:* Gall, brazen, nerve.
"It takes *chutzpah* to initiate conversations."
RoAne's usage: Courage, gutsiness.
"The crook embezzles from the company and then requests a farewell party! That's *chutzpah!*"

(Cyber)dreck Trash, junk, that of inferior quality; a vulgar term not to use around my mother—or yours.

"When the *Wall Street Journal* has described some of what is available in cyberspace as cyberdreck, it must really be awful!"

253

Fe! or Feh! An exclamatory expression of disgust and distaste.

"They are serving pasta with scallops and kumquats? *Feh!*"

Kvell To beam with immense pride and pleasure.

"The happy parents were *kvelling* at their son's bar mitzvah."

Kvetch To fuss, gripe, complain. The person who does that.

"Brenda is constantly *kvetching* about everything."

Maven An expert, knowledgeable person.

"With the new portable phones, the manners mavens have their work cut out for them."

Mazel tov! Good luck, congratulations.

"I am so pleased that you were promoted. *Mazel tov!*"

Megillah Anything long, complicated, boring.

"Tell me the results of the negotiations. I don't want to hear the whole *megillah.*"

Mensch An honorable person of integrity; someone of noble character with a sense of sweetness as well as what is right and responsible. To call someone a *mensch* reflects deep respect.

"Dan Donovan, my stockbroker, is a real *mensch!*"

Nosh To eat in between meals. A snack, a small portion, a nibble.

"Cousin Shelly prefers to *nosh* and nibble all day than to eat three meals."

Nudge To pester, nag; to give a surreptitious reminder of a job to be done. The person who is a nag.
"He kept on nudging her to stop smoking."

Oy vay! A lament, a protest or a cry of delight. It expresses anguish, joy, pain, revulsion, regret, relief.
"*Oy vay!* It is such a tragedy to lose a home in a fire. Thank heaven the family is safe."

Schlep To drag, pull or lag behind. Someone who looks bedraggled and *schleppish*.
"Don't *schlep* all those packages, you'll hurt your back."

Schmooze Friendly and gossipy, prolonged conversation; act of chatting *with* someone.
"Ira and Michael schmoozed for an hour at the party."
Incorrect: "Ira schmoozed Michael at the party."

Schnorrer A cheapskate, a chiseler.
"Talk about timing, that *schnorrer* Barbara always manages to be in the rest room when the bill arrives."

Shivah The seven solemn days of mourning for the dead when Jews "sit *shivah*" in the home of the deceased.
"During my father's *shivah*, relatives, friends and his business associates from his sixty-four years in the paper industry came to pay their respects."

Shtick A studied, contrived piece of "business" employed by an actor (or salesperson); a trick; a devious trick.
"Watch him use the same *shtick* on this new client."

Tush Derriere (a cute term); bottomed out.
"One cannot work a room on one's tush."

Yenta *Classic definition:* A gossipy woman who does not keep a secret. It may also refer to a man who does the same.

Newer usage: Since *Fiddler on the Roof,* a matchmaker. "I do expect that someday we'll sing 'Networker, Networker . . . make me a match, Yenta.'"

BIBLIOGRAPHY

ARTICLES

Boyd, Robert, and Dr. Barry Gordon. Cited in "Memory: Remembering and Forgetting in Everyday Life." *Marin Independent Journal,* March 31, 1996.

Burrus, Daniel. *Professional Speaker.* National Speakers Association, Phoenix, January/February 1996.

Keyfitz, Nathan. "The Baby Boom Meets the Computer Revolution." *American Demographics,* May 1984, pp. 23–25, 45–46.

Dame Raquel. "Netiquette Diva." *Wired,* various 1995.

RoAne, Susan. "Fed Up with Feedback or Who Asked You Anyway?" *Meeting Manager.* MPI, Dallas, July 1987.

Stettner, Morey. "Learning to Master the Art of Interruptions." *Investors Business Daily,* Vol. 12, No. 224, p. 1.

BOOKS

Alessandra, Tony, Ph.D. *The Platinum Rule.* New York: Warner Books, 1996.

Branden, Nathaniel, Ph.D. *The Six Pillars of Self-Esteem.* New York: Bantam, 1994.

Briles, Judith. *GenderTraps.* New York: McGraw-Hill, 1996.

Burrus, Daniel. *Technotrends.* New York: Harper Business, 1994.

Byrne, Robert. *The 637 Best Things Anybody Ever Said.* New York: Fawcett Crest, 1981.

———. *The Other 637 Best Things Anybody Ever Said.* New York: Fawcett Crest, 1984.

———. *The Third and Possibly the 637 Best Things Anybody Ever Said.* New York: Fawcett Crest, 1986.

Cialdini, Robert, Ph.D. *Influence: The New Psychology of Modern Persuasion.* New York: Quill, 1984.

Ekman, Paul. *Telling Lies.* Magnolia, MA: Peter Smith, 1993.

Feld, Bruce, and Christine Evatt. *The Givers and The Takers.* New York: Macmillan Collier, 1983.

Goleman, Daniel. *Emotional Intelligence.* New York: Bantam, 1995.

Horn, Sam. *Tongue Fu!* New York: St. Martin's Press, 1996.

Kennedy, Marilyn Moats. *Office Politics: Seizing Power, Wielding Clout.* Chicago: Follett, 1980.

Lewis, David. *The Secret Language of Success.* New York: Carroll & Graf, 1986.

Lonier, Terri. *Working Solo.* New Paltz, NY: Portico Press, 1994.

Mandell, Terri. *Power Shmoozing.* New York: McGraw-Hill, 1996.

McCullough, Christopher, Ph.D. *Always at Ease.* New York: Berkley, 1993.

————. *Managing Your Anxiety.* Los Angeles: Jeremy Tarcher, 1985.

Negroponte, Nicholas. *Being Digital.* New York: Alfred A. Knopf, 1995.

RoAne, Susan. *How to Work a™ Room.* New York: Warner Books, 1989.

————. *The Secrets of Savvy Networking.* New York: Warner Books, 1993.

Robertson, Jeanne. *Humor: The Magic of Genie.* Houston, TX: Rich Publishing, 1990.

Rosten, Leo. *The Joys of Yiddish.* New York: Washington Square Press, 1968.

Scheele, Adele, Ph.D. *Skills for Success.* New York: Ballantine, 1987.

Bibliography

Tannen, Deborah, Ph.D. *Talking from 9 to 5.* New York: Morrow, 1994.

———. *That's Not What I Meant.* New York: Ballantine, 1985.

Yudkin, Marcia. *On-Line Marketing.* New York: Plume, 1995.

Williams, Terrie. *The Personal Touch.* New York: Warner Books, 1994.

Zimbardo, Philip, Ph.D. *Shyness: What It Is, What to Do About It.* New York: Addison-Wesley, 1977.

INDEX

Index

Index

Index